The Zone

An Alternative History of Paris

Justinien Tribillon

VERSO

London • New York

First published by Verso 2024
© Justinien Tribillon 2024

1 3 5 7 9 10 8 6 4 2

Verso
UK: 6 Meard Street, London W1F 0EG
US: 388 Atlantic Avenue, Brooklyn, NY 11217
versobooks.com

Verso is the imprint of New Left Books

ISBN-13: 978-1-80429-404-8
ISBN-13: 978-1-80429-407-9 (US EBK)
ISBN-13: 978-1-80429-406-2 (UK EBK)

British Library Cataloguing in Publication Data
A catalogue record for this book is available from the British Library

Library of Congress Cataloging-in-Publication Data

Names: Tribillon, Justinien, author.
Title: The zone : an alternative history of Paris / Justinien Tribillon.
Description: London ; New York : Verso, 2024. | Includes bibliographical
  references and index. | Summary: "In The Zone, Justinien Tribillon takes
  the reader on a tour of an eponymous Parisian hinterland"-- Provided by
  publisher.
Identifiers: LCCN 2024000556 (print) | LCCN 2024000557 (ebook) | ISBN
  9781804294048 (hardback) | ISBN 9781804294079 (ebook)
Subjects: LCSH: Paris (France)--History. | Paris Region (France)--History.
  | Suburbs--France--Paris--History. | City
  planning--France--Paris--History. | Paris (France)--Social conditions. |
  Paris (France)--Description and travel. | City
  walls--France--Paris--History.
Classification: LCC DC768 .T75 2024 (print) | LCC DC768 (ebook) | DDC
  944/.361--dc23/eng/20240213
LC record available at https://lccn.loc.gov/2024000556
LC ebook record available at https://lccn.loc.gov/2024000557

Typeset in Fournier MT by Hewer Text UK Ltd, Edinburgh
Printed and bound by CPI Group (UK) Ltd, Croydon CR0 4YY

MIX
Paper | Supporting
responsible forestry
FSC® C171272

Contents

For Cécile

Introduction

It is an ugly wall built in a rush, with fresh mortar drooling over the bare breeze blocks. On the branded hard hats of the construction workers, a stylised sun rising over the brightest blue skies. On normal days, they are posted on the Grand Paris Express building sites, the major expansion of the regional railway network for the Paris region. But today they have sealed off a foot tunnel under the Boulevard Périphérique, the ring road of Paris, surrounded by police officers in bulletproof vests, with guns in holsters that they wear high on their thighs.

In the early hours of that same day, Friday, 24 September 2021, the police cleared the surroundings of Rue Riquet in the eighteenth arrondissement of Paris, rounding up a population of crack users that had settled down there and busing them to a tiny garden right by the ring road, at Porte de la Villette. The story repeats itself over the years. Before Rue Riquet, they camped out in slum-like conditions at Porte de la Chapelle, on the *colline du crack* ('crack hill') until its dismantlement by the police at the end of 2019.

The prefect of police of Paris, Didier Lallement, explained the choice of Porte de la Villette, saying there were 'no neighbours in the

immediate vicinity' of the park. It is true there are very few immediate
neighbours on Paris's side. But the first residential buildings are a mere
three-minute walk from the makeshift camp, located in the suburban
towns of Pantin and Aubervilliers, in the *département* of Seine-Saint-
Denis. Inhabitants there cannot see the camp from their windows –
what they see is the ring road viaduct. Nor can they hear the cries at
night – these are deafened by the sound of traffic. But they now have
to bear the public health and safety burden of their new Parisian
neighbours.

What has angered residents of the newly nicknamed *quartier de la
défonce* (the 'get-stoned district', a paronomasia referring to the business district of La Défense, west of Paris) and their elected officials
was not only that people struggling with drug addiction were moved
into their neighbourhood and settled in an open-air camp with no
infrastructure to host and help them. They were also angered by the
total absence of consultation or even advanced warning by the prefect
of Paris, and the extra insult of a double wall erected on the same day,
to provide an 'indispensable protection to inhabitants of Pantin',
according to the prefect.

Until September 2021, a pedestrian underpass under the ring
road connected Pantin to Paris and Paris to Pantin, an extension of
the Rue Berthier that was severed in 1964 to make space for the
motorway. Many have interpreted the abrupt closure of the crossing
on both sides as a stark display of Parisian disdain for the inhabitants of Seine-Saint-Denis. And for their elected officials, it was
flouting their democratic legitimacy. As for the mayor of Paris,
Anne Hidalgo, she had indeed called on the government to clear
Rue Riquet, but later declared that she was unaware of the evacua-
tion and eventually criticised it as being a mere spatial displacement
of the problem and not a tenable solution.

The Wall of Shame, at the border between Paris, Pantin
and Aubervilliers. A few days after its construction.

Commentators, officials and residents denounced the prefect's decision to move the group of crack users to one of France's poorest neighbourhoods for no valid reason, instead of picking more appropriate sites
in the south or the affluent west of Paris.[1] The decision is typical of a
certain simplistic (or hypocritical) administrative bird's-eye view
understanding of Paris and its boundaries: the blocking of the foot
tunnel under the ring road does very little to protect the inhabitants of
Pantin. One needs to walk only fifty metres to the Place Auguste
Baron, then continue around the piles of the ring road viaduct and past
the Portuguese market of La Villette to arrive in Pantin, surrounded
by housing, cafés, chemists, nurseries, schools, libraries and so on.
The wall is stronger as a symbol than as a protective measure.

Within days, the 'crack wall' or 'wall of shame', as it has been
dubbed, was covered with graffiti, and a demonstration was organised

by Seine-Saint-Denis's elected officials – to no avail. In January 2022, a project to move drug users again, this time to a brownfield site owned by the SNCF, France's public railway company, in the much more bourgeois twelfth arrondissement, was almost immediately dropped after Parisian councillors from all parties, who had been consulted in advance, protested vehemently.

There is another side to that story, one that sleeps in the city archives. In March 1953, the Council of Paris granted a lease to the city of Pantin to enable it to build the Park Jean Jaurès on the Porte de la Villette. Since the land had been earmarked for the ring road, the precarious nature of this lease was specifically mentioned to the mayor of Pantin, who was afterwards regularly reminded of this fact by the prefecture of the Seine. The garden seems to have been a popular spot for the population of Pantin and the city's only green space at the time. However, in November 1959, when the Council of Paris voted to fund the building of the section of ring road that would run through Porte de la Villette, and the Communist mayor of Pantin received a notification to clear the park by January 1961 to make way for construction, he protested and demanded that the ring road design be modified. Naturally, his endeavour failed, and in 1964 the garden was destroyed.

But in exchange, the prefect promised to replace the two-hectare park with a smaller, 1.4-hectare one, the Square de la Porte de la Villette, and to build a foot tunnel to allow easy access from Pantin to the *square* on the south side of the ring road. This space was, so to speak, a leftover, as the ring road path made a curve over Porte de la Villette. When the prefect of police of Paris, acting on orders from Minister of the Interior Gérald Darmanin, decided in 2021 to make the tiny garden of Porte de la Villette an open-air camp for a population suffering from crack addiction and sealed off the foot tunnel between Pantin and the park, it was the second time that the central state had robbed Pantin residents of a public space. History repeats itself for good reason.

When I give talks about the urban planning of Paris to a non-francophone audience, I like to start by listing the French words and expressions that attendees can come up with: from *bonjour* to *Voulez-vous coucher avec moi, ce soir?*, from *croissant* to *Je n'ai pas compris*, from *Moulin Rouge* to *banlieue*. This has always fascinated me: in which other languages can you say 'suburbs'? Would you come up with *Vorort* in German or *sobborgo* in Italian?

Paris is a myth known the world over. A global beacon of beauty, elegance, intelligence, culture, refinement, romanticism. It has been painted by the greatest, photographed by the most talented, described by the most gifted, visited by the most illustrious, loved by the grandest. There are millions of representations of Paris across the globe: it lives in Palermo, pinned on a teenager's bedroom wall, saving up for the big trip. In the dining room of a Mexico City retirement home. On the dashboard of a Malian taxi driver picking you up at the Modibo Keita International Airport of Bamako. Taped on the sliding toilet door of a flat in Kyoto. Hung above the clock in a train station in Kerala. Dangling from a keyring shoved in the front pocket of a backpack in Houston, Texas.

That the actual Paris, the Paris I know, is a vile, dirty, stinky, feral, exhausting, pushy, aggressive city does not matter. That it is a city of immense energy and violence, that it spits on your face, kicks you in the butt, leaves you in the gutter – all of this does not matter. Because Paris is an idea, a dream, a desire.

We rarely acknowledge that the banlieue of Paris is a mythical space too. It is more remote, allusive, less tangible than postcard Paris. It is made of an artistic blur, mostly negative, that usually includes high-rise modernist towers, the characters of *La Haine* (1995) and *Athena* (2022), violence and cars on fire, or even the association of the 'no-go zones'. When using the word *banlieue*, we – may that 'we' be from France or from any country in the world – rarely include the posh suburbs, the likes of Neuilly-sur-Seine in the west and Saint-Maurice in the east, or the modest, often patched-up detached houses that constitute the vast majority of Paris's banlieue urban fabric. In French, *banlieue* is often used as a singular instead of a plural, removing the diversity of architectures, socio-economic contexts, histories and communities who live there. The banlieue is a single entity, a block. Finally, the word *banlieue* is often used with a possessive – it is Paris's banlieue, a territory of 10 million souls acting as a servicing excrescence for the city *proper* of 2.5 million.

Paris and banlieue are two mythical and geographical spaces that have been constructed in opposition. Their histories are entangled, to form a complex mass made of design choices, social policy, colonialism, immigration, administrative rulings, models of policing and 'peacekeeping', fear and hatred. The opposition between Paris and the surrounding suburbs crystallises around a specific space: the Zone. This borderland, an in-between space that divides the outer limits of Paris and the inner boundaries of the banlieue, creates a stark spatial demarcation between the 'in' and the 'out', the 'us' and the 'them', Paris and the Other.

In this book, I will examine this constructed opposition between Paris proper and the banlieue by way of the Zone. Because to understand Paris, you need to hear the voices of the Zone.

In French, Paris proper is referred to as Paris *intramuros*, a Latin expression meaning 'within the wall'. Since the late nineteenth century, the outer edges of Paris proper have been weaponised to mark off the bourgeois city from its working-class suburbs. For instance, from the 1840s until the 1920s, a two-hundred-metre-deep military wall and a series of forts surrounded the city; from 1790 until 1943, a tax on goods was levied upon entering Paris; and from the 1840s until 1940s, an in-between area with complex legal status hosted informal housing, light industries, cabarets and theatres all around the limits of the city.

The majority of the Zone was cleared by the Vichy regime to build the ring road, with portions of it surviving well into the 1970s. Constructed between 1956 and 1973, the Boulevard Périphérique itself is the epitome of the technocratic urban planning of the Fifth Republic, designed and erected at a time when Parisians were not allowed to elect their mayor. Indeed, from 1794 to 1977, Paris was the only French city under tutelage from the state. It was headed by a prefect, a civil servant appointed by the national government, for fear that a mayor backed by the people of Paris would be too powerful and uncontrollable. Indeed, the last one had ruled for just a few months when the Parisians revolted against the national government during the Commune of 1871.

The space of Paris is therefore layered with the decrees, policies and laws, imposed not by democratically elected mayors, but by civil servants, prefects, ministers, kings and presidents. Infused with moral principles, political motives, racism and lucre, Paris is made of prejudices and intolerance for its people.

By way of a walk along the ring road of Paris, this book proposes to read the city from the outside inwards. Across five chapters, I will take you on five belts, at times physical and metaphorical: the black belt of the Zone inhabited by the ragpickers, artists and blue-collar workers; a green belt designed as a buffer between the city proper and the suburbs to protect the interests of Parisian landlords; the Red Belt of Communist cities threatening to take control of bourgeois Paris; the dirt belt of the ring road itself imagined by the Parisian technocracy; and the rust belt of the *bidonvilles* and the *cités*, a journey into colonial Paris and the 'margins of the empire'. From ruins to shiny office buildings, from the ghosts of Vincennes to the bustling flea market of Saint-Ouen, from the defeats of Napoleon to the presidential archives of Charles de Gaulle, let us walk the most unknown yet quintessentially Parisian space: the Zone.

1

Black Belt: Creating an Edge

A VHS of *Rambo* for one euro, worn-out Adidas running shoes, a 1980s baby phone missing the receiver, a small mound of clothes thrown on the pavement, a rusted drill, six bolts – a Nokia 3310, twelve iPhones of different models spanning as many years, a Dolce Gusto espresso machine with limescale on it, two old jigsaws, one screw-gun, fourteen electric drills (six Bosch, three DeWalt, one Kärcher, four Makita) covered with bits of paint and plaster, a male doll with no pants on, a one-foot-high pile of clothes on a piece of tarpaulin with four people rummaging through it, a Michelin guide from 1998, an electric handheld massager in its original box, an Elmo cuddly toy, three salvaged faucets, a Discman, a two-part installation CD-ROM for Mac OS X, a book of haikus by Matsuo Bashō translated into French, a lava lamp (a copy) – a collection of rugs, cleaning products (new) and sweets (new as well) neatly organised on picnic folding tables, (fake) Louis Vuitton bags, branded sunglasses, genuine Canada Goose coats, Nike streetwear, cartons of Marlboros, Louis Aragon's complete works, an Apple watch in its original unopened box that a guy takes out of a black plastic bag, perfumes – postcards organised by theme and geographical location, vintage clothes (Yves Saint-Laurent, Vivienne Westwood, Jean-Paul Gaultier), shabby-chic furniture, a collection of *Paris Match* magazines protected by plastic pockets and organised by year of publication: twenty euros a piece – Nazi memorabilia, a cutesy shop that sells only vintage enamel coffee pots, china, a one-to-one replica of Rodin's *Thinker* in a shop that sells sculptures for gardens, a portrait of Émile Zola by Nadar (an original), a genuine Charles and Ray Eames rocking chair, a four-hundred-year-old Samurai armour set made by Myochin Fujihiza with a price tag of €43,000, a *Compression of Garden Chairs* by César: €95K.

Unlike other global cities that have expanded and sprawled until their edges disappeared in the distance, Paris has well-identified thresholds that determine who is *in* and who is *out*. The thresholds of Paris are spatial but not only that – they are social, cultural and political too. The flea markets, such as the *puces* of Saint-Ouen, on the edges of the city proper, are the expression of such thresholds.

Two thousand sellers spread out over an area the size of ten football pitches. In the last two decades or so, the 'official' *puces* has become a spot more for tourists than for bargains. Known for its overpriced antiques, the market is a destination for interior designers working for clients with deep pockets, and bohemians who want to experience the thrill of buying a vintage Eileen Gray table or a lamp that looks like this-designer-you-know-the-one-I-mean-okay-let-me-google-it, so much so that they will pay twice as much as it is worth elsewhere. The official *puces* prides itself in its 5 million visitors, 'including many celebrities', and is organised around covered indoor *marchés* – Biron, Cambo, Dauphine, Malassis and so on. The atmosphere is sophisticated: merchants coolly wait for their *clientèle* dressed in fur coats and sat in authentic Scandinavian chairs, price tags contain several zeros and are whispered in French or English, Russian and Chinese, while chauffeured Mercedes await their masters and mistresses outside.

Now leave the posh *puces* and walk a few minutes until you reach Rue Jean-Henri Fabre, named after one of the founding figures of entomology – the perfect toponymy for a flea market. Here and by Porte de Clignancourt, the *puces* offers an entirely different atmosphere. Stalls line up for half a kilometre, from the Avenue Michelet down to Rue Paul Schmidt. They lean against the ring road, with cars driving by at high speed a couple of metres away.

It is rare to be so close to the Boulevard Périphérique, with so little protection, almost no buffer. While on Paris's side, soundproof walls limit the impact of noise from the ring road, there is nothing here to protect Saint-Ouen from the sonic waves that crash on its residential buildings. For ten years now I have walked, studied, photographed and wrote about the edges of Paris and the relation the capital city has with the surrounding banlieue. And yet the tragic and grotesque injustice between Paris and the myriad of suburban towns surrounding it keeps baffling me. Paris gets protection, while Saint-Ouen is left naked.

Along Rue Jean-Henri Fabre, you will find mainly clothes – counterfeit and genuine, good bargains either way. The garments here are mostly new, not vintage. French is spoken, but the most prevalent language is Arabic (with speakers from Tunisia, Morocco and Algeria). It is about nine in the morning; stalls have just opened, but the market is bustling. The air is cold and crisp, the sun is about to come out from behind the morning haze of pollution and everyone can expect a good weekend of trading.

As you progress towards Porte Montmartre, the stands start to offer goods you could find in any working-class neighbourhood

markets in France: cheap products at wholesale price and in large
quantities (two litres of bleach, Milka chocolate bars sold by packs of
ten, one-kilogram jars of Nutella, five-litre jerrican of white vinegar).
At the end of the street, the selection of goods progressively develops
to include secondhand merchandise picked with care and organised
on folding tables in a conscientious and appealing way: cameras, old
books, photographs and some cheap furniture. Then at Porte
Montmartre, another world starts.

You enter the kingdom of the *biffins* or the *chiffoniers* – literally, the
ragpickers or rag-and-bone (wo)men. Going through people's
garbage, they salvage anything that could have some value. The
market was formalised in 2009 by city hall, and officially circumscribed to this space beneath the ring road. There is a bright winter
sun now, but here the market will remain dark. The concrete around
us has been blackened by the exhaust fumes, and the shouts of the sellers – bargains, banter, the odd argument – echo under the deck of the
Périph that passes above our heads.

The selection here is less appealing and presented with little care,
but if you are patient and savvy enough you will find great buys. The
'rags' sold at Porte Montmartre – from clothes to old phones – compose
a portrait of Parisians by way of their garbage. Think Arcimboldo's
painting but made of filth. The sellers' faces are tired and wrinkled.
Chiffonier is a tough trade, one of last resort. These men and women
woke up early or stayed up late to rummage through Paris's bins and
glean what could be gleaned before the tipper came to collect it all.

The flea market does not end there. A short walk away from the
formal *biffins*, on Rue Louis Pasteur Valléry-Radot, nested between
social housing *cités* and a brand-new 'boutique' hotel, is the unofficial
satellite of the rag-and-bone market. Twenty or thirty people have
placed themselves in line, every metre or so. Even more than the flea

market, more than the official *biffins*, here is a market for outsiders, by outsiders. An expression of poverty, and like most expressions of deprivation, of extreme resilience. When the market comes to an end, at the beginning of the afternoon, sellers often leave their goods there, to be cleared out by the *propreté de Paris*, the city's cleaners. If no one bought it today, no one ever will.

From rags to riches, from Porte Montmartre to the posh market halls of the *puces*, the flea market of Saint-Ouen located on the edges of Paris is a highly concentrated expression of the social, political and ethno-racial geography of Paris: extreme poverty sits next to extravagant wealth, the former made up mostly of working-class (first-, second- or third-generation) immigrants from Africa and Asia, the latter comprising predominantly white tourists.

Chiffoniers, *biffins*, *crocheteurs*, *chtifires*, or *pêcheurs de lune* – 'moon anglers' – and their markets, the *puces*, have a long history intertwined with the space of Paris. The formal and informal flea markets of Saint-Ouen, Montreuil and Vanves, are the continuation of socio-economic practice dating back centuries. By their presence, they perpetuate a space that has occupied the edges of the city limits since the nineteenth century: the Zone.

The twenty-ninth of March 1814. Napoleon's armies were on the brink of collapse. After the catastrophic Campaign of Russia in 1812, and the lost Battle of Leipzig in October 1813, the French troops retreated across Germany into France, pursued by the Sixth Coalition formed of Russia, Prussia, Austria, Netherlands, Bavaria, Sweden, Switzerland, Britain, Spain and Portugal. The coalition forces arrived in the suburbs of the imperial capital city, set for battle the day after. The men of the Prussian field marshal Gebhard Leberecht von Blücher attacked the north of the city, an arc from Clichy to La Villette that included Saint-Denis, Montmartre, Aubervilliers and La Chapelle. General Barclay, a Russian aristocrat of Scottish origin, was in charge of storming Pantin and Montreuil.

From Charenton to Vincennes, in the southeast, the Prince of Württemberg had his soldiers march across the Bois de Vincennes. By 6:30 p.m., the fighting that started twelve hours before had stopped. By 2 a.m. the next day, the French Army had formally surrendered. And at 7 a.m. on 31 March the coalition forces entered Paris by the Porte Saint-Martin, marching under a triumphal arch built by Louis XIV in 1674. The arch is still in place today, at the crossroad of Rue Saint-Martin and the *grands boulevards*; its seventeenth-century bas-reliefs ironically represent the 'Defeat of the Germans' and the 'Breaking of the Triple Alliance' (formed by England, Sweden and the Dutch Republic). A few days later Napoleon abdicated and was exiled to the Isle of Elba, off the coast of Tuscany.

But just eleven months later, on 20 March 1815, Napoleon was back in Paris. In February, he had escaped from Italy, landed next to Antibes and marched towards Paris, reconstituting his army as soldiers rallied his cause. This Napoleonic comeback was eventually crushed at the Battle of Waterloo on 18 June 1815, and the story repeated itself: the Seventh Coalition besieged the capital city and won the Battle of Issy, a suburban town southwest of Paris. Napoleon capitulated and the generals in charge of defending the city surrendered Paris to Prince Blücher and the Duke of Wellington on 3 July 1815. For the second time in less than two years, Paris was lost, and the coalition forces entered the capital city victoriously. Paris was humiliated, and France's pride scorned. In the minds of French military elites, the resolution started to settle in: the 'head and heart of the kingdom', Paris, needed a major overhaul of its defence system.

⚜

Paris has been bounded by a series of walls acting as administrative and fiscal boundaries as well as military infrastructure since the fourth century. At first it was a fortified Île de la Cité, 'City Island', where Notre Dame is located today. Then a medieval wall on the right bank of the Seine River went up to the present-day Louvre, Centre Pompidou and City Hall. In the twelfth century, Philip II Augustus ordered the construction of a new fortified wall to protect Paris from the English before he left for the Crusades. Three kilometres long on each bank and eight to ten metres high, it increased the surface area of the fortified town and went up to present-day Jardin du Luxembourg in the south, the Halles district in the north and today's Place des Vosges in the east.

In the second half of the sixteenth century, the fortifications on the *rive droite*, the north bank of the Seine, were upgraded as an answer to 'the crisis of the metallic ball', as it was nicknamed by contemporaries. Cannonballs changed the rules of warfare. Bastions were added to the fortified wall, as well as dry moats. The building works to reinforce the wall surrounding Paris that had been started in the 1550s were almost complete in 1670 when Louis XIV, in a complete U-turn, changed the kingdom's defence strategy entirely. He declared Paris an open city and ordered the fortifications dismantled. He focused instead on reinforcing the borders of his kingdom, entrusting the engineer Vauban to erect forts all around the country's edges.

By 1700, there was nothing left of the fortified wall in Paris. The fortifications and ditches were redesigned as *nouveau cours*, new avenues for promenading – today the boulevards connecting Place de la Bastille, to Place de la République, and then the beginning of the *grands boulevards*. The limits between the then city proper and its continuation past the fortifications are still present in the street names – for instance, when Rue Saint-Denis becomes Rue du Faubourg-Saint-Denis, *faubourg* being an archaic name for suburb.

At the same time, the Crown, which struggled to organise the collection of taxes, decided to 'outsource' it to an ad-hoc company: the Company of the General Farm, created in 1680. Indeed, a fiscal boundary separated Paris, where a tax known as *octroi* was due, and the surrounding countryside that paid the *taille*, a land tax. All thoroughfares entering Paris had a barrier, a shed and a gate, where tariff was due. But fraud was prevalent, and in 1785 the company commissioned Claude-Nicolas Ledoux, the most inspiring architect of a generation, to erect a wall surrounding the city, along with grand toll houses.

As with most of Ledoux's legendary designs, few of his Parisian toll houses survive today – the Rotunda at La Villette by the Canal Saint-Martin is one of those. Completed in 1790, the wall was despised by Parisians. The poet, playwright, businessman and spy Pierre Caron de Beaumarchais summed up these sentiments in a famous alexandrine in alliteration: 'Le mur murant Paris rend Paris murmurant' (The wall walling Paris makes Paris grumble). There is also this anonymous epigram: 'To amass more money / And shorten our horizon / The Farm found it necessary / To put Paris in a prison.'

One metre deep, three metres high and twenty-four kilometres long, the Wall of the General Farm was not a military fortification but a fiscal threshold and an administrative boundary. Its path followed approximatively that of lines 2 and 6 of the *métro* today. The wall was removed in the nineteenth century but the tax on goods entering Paris remained in place until August 1943. This meant that until 1943, if you left the city with, say, your car's tank half empty and came back with the tank full to the brim with petrol, you theoretically had to pay taxes on that extra fuel.

⚜

Following the two humiliating defeats of 1814 and 1815, in which Paris had surrendered within less than twenty-four hours, the debate about building a defensive wall – which had not completely stopped since Louis XIV decided to de-fortify Paris – was revived. Two main designs were in opposition: the first proposed the construction of a continuous wall surrounding the city, able to hold back invading armies while waiting for reinforcements. The second project was a continuous wall backed up by a constellation of detached forts located in the suburbs. Other questions arose: did Paris need to fortify the Wall of the General Farm or build entirely new infrastructure further away from Paris proper?

At the time, Paris was circumscribed to an area that included today's first twelve arrondissements. Montmartre, La Villette,

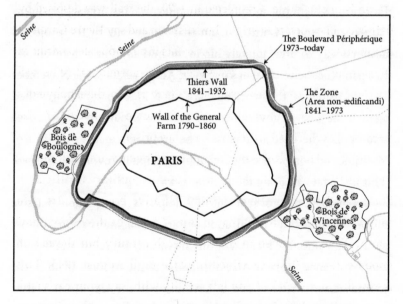

Map representing the boundaries of Paris proper today, the Wall of the General Farm, the Zone, the Wall of Thiers, the Boulevard Périphérique and the Bois de Vincennes and Bois de Boulogne.

Ménilmontant, Bercy, La Chapelle and Vaugirard were independent towns outside the Wall of the General Farm. The territories of present-day suburban towns such as Charenton, Saint-Denis and Gentilly went up to the fiscal and administrative boundary of Paris. The debate was about military strategy and local politics – would Paris swallow its neighbours? – but there was another concern: was this wall about fighting off invading armies or controlling the riotous people of Paris?

For that reason, the poet and politician Alphonse de Lamartine was fiercely opposed to the scheme he deemed 'counterrevolutionary'. The wall was a way to kill the Revolution, he argued. Another vehement opponent to the new wall was François Arago – the mathematician, astronomer and politician who would become president of France in 1848 for one month. The architectural historians Jean-Louis Cohen and André Lortie explain that Arago saw in the projected design a way to preemptively nip in the bud any Parisian rebellion.[1] In a pamphlet he wrote that same year, Arago refers to the November 1842 uprising of the working classes of Barcelona who revolted against the liberal government of General Espartero and the free trade policy he tried to impose. The army retreated to the fort of Montjuïc and bombarded the city until the popular revolt was crushed. This is the fate awaiting the Parisians, warned Arago.

Yet in 1840, the government of Adolphe Thiers made a decisive move to construct the fortification of Paris, using international tumult as a justification. Thiers was an important figure of nineteenth-century France. Born in Marseille and arriving in Paris in 1821, the journalist and writer is said to have inspired the Honoré de Balzac character Rastignac, the archetypal amoral, power-hungry young provincial man who moves to Paris with unlimited ambition. Author of a best-selling history of the 1789 French Revolution, Thiers became an MP in 1830, then minister for finance the same year, then minister of the interior in 1832 and again in 1834.

He had made a reputation for himself as an enemy of the people when he harshly repressed the workers' revolt in Paris and in Lyon in April 1834. In Paris, where Thiers on horseback personally led the repression, the army stormed a building on Rue Transnonain, where protesters had found refuge, and massacred twelve residents including women, children and the elderly. While in Lyon, Thiers tested a strategy he would later reuse against the Paris Commune of 1871: he ordered the troops to retreat from the city streets and, from the outside, besieged it without mercy, killing 276.

In March 1840, 'Foutriquet', or 'Pipsqueak' – as the people mockingly nicknamed five-foot-tall Thiers – became head of the government. Despised by the Parisians following the Massacre of the Rue Transnonain, he used the signature of an international treaty as a pretext to go ahead with his plan to fortify Paris. The Convention of London, signed in July 1840 between the United Kingdom, Russia, Prussia and Austria, was a commitment to support the Ottoman Empire against Muhammad Ali, viceroy and pasha of Egypt, the latter supported by France. In this treaty, Thiers saw the threat of a new alliance against France.

But Thiers only used the Oriental Crisis as an excuse to build the wall in an effort to restrict Parisians' civil liberties.[2] In a letter dated 17 July 1833, François Arago criticised the new wall and denounced *l'embastillement de Paris*, a neologism referring to the infamous Bastille prison-cum-fortress. The expression came back to the fore as the Thiers Wall was about to turn Paris into an open-air prison. On 10 September 1840, a royal ordinance declared the fortification of *utilité publique*, meaning the project was granted special benefits to facilitate its completion.

Three days later, the government approved the emergency credits and construction started immediately. A month later, Thiers's government fell. His successor, General Soult, drafted a bill to retroactively allocate 140 million francs to the project. By the time the bill was approved by both chambers of the parliament in April 1841, construction was well underway. The 'Thiers Wall', as it was immediately named, was completed just four years later.

At a time when European cities were decommissioning their city walls, confident that the nature of warfare had changed, Paris built a new one. Erected 2 kilometres away from the Wall of the General Farm, the Thiers Wall constituted an imposing piece of military infrastructure. Starting from the inside, it comprised a 6-metre cobbled rampart walk, an embankment and a 10-metre-high, 3.5-metre-deep fortress wall reinforced by abutments every 5 metres, while the external 40-metre-large ditch was followed by a 250-metre-deep strip of land *non-ædificandi*, where construction was forbidden. Totaling 400 metres deep and 34 kilometres long, the Thiers Wall occupied a surface area of 1,200 hectares, or 15 per cent of the city's territory. The landscape of Paris was transformed by the wall. Paris proper was granted a new name: Paris *intramuros*, literally translated as Paris 'walled-in'. Paris *intramuros* remains the idiomatic appellation for Paris proper today; the memory of the wall lives on.

Despite the massive military wall, the city's administrative and fiscal boundaries remained where the Wall of the General Farm, freshly deconstructed, once stood. The octroi was due not upon crossing the Thiers wall but once you had reached present-day Place de la Nation, or Place Denfert-Rochereau (known as Barrière d'Enfer, or 'Hell's Gates'), or Place de l'Étoile and its Arc de

Triomphe, erected just a few years prior in 1836. While they formally retained control over them, the suburban towns adjacent to Paris had seen a portion of their territories disappear *behind* Thiers's wall, with the successive governments promising that they had no intention to expand the capital city's limits up to the fortifications.

The year 1848. Another revolution. Another republic, the second. Louis-Napoléon Bonaparte, Napoleon's nephew, was elected president of France on 10 December 1848 – the first election of its kind in France. This attempt at democracy did not last, however. Looking up to his revered uncle, Bonaparte quickly dissolved the republic and anointed himself Napoleon III, 'Emperor of the French'. Inspired by Victoria's London, where he had lived for many years, 'Napoleon the small', or 'Little Caesar', as his opponent the exiled writer Victor Hugo mockingly nicknamed the politician, had grand plans for Paris urbanism. In 1853, he appointed Georges-Eugène Haussmann as prefect of the Seine, the then name of the administrative entity that included Paris and towns of the suburbs.

To this day, Baron Haussmann remains one of the most (in)famous figures in the history of urbanism. From his nomination until the fall of the Second Empire and his dismissal in 1870, Haussmann led an intensive enterprise to reshape and 'strategically embellish' Paris. In his essay 'Paris, Capital of the 19th Century', which formed the preparatory work for his uncompleted *Arcades Project*, Walter Benjamin analyses the reshaping of Paris as a counterinsurgent design to prevent revolting Parisians from blocking the progress of loyalist military forces by building barricades across the street. Ten years after the construction of the Thiers Wall which, for its opponents, had *embastillé* the Parisians, Haussmann made urban planning serve Napoleon III's antidemocratic and antisocial political project.

A few weeks before he betrayed the Second Republic, President Bonaparte had publicly reaffirmed that the area concerned with the collection of the octroi would not be extended up to the Thiers Wall and that the City of Paris would not be, de facto, enlarged. Just a few years later, the deceptive autocrat and his administration had changed their position. Despite the virulent opposition by elected officials and the population, who were consulted but not heard, as the historian Nathalie Montel demonstrated, the extension of Paris was promulgated in November 1859 and effective from 1 January 1860.[3] The annexation meant that from the first day of 1860, eleven municipalities disappeared totally to be incorporated into Paris as neighbourhoods: Grenelle, Belleville, La Villette, Vaugirard, Auteuil, Batignolles-Monceau, Bercy, Charonne, La Chapelle, Montmartre and Passy. And the territories of nine other towns were amputated as some of their districts were also annexed to the city: Neuilly, Le Pré Saint-Gervais, Pantin, Saint-Mandé, Ivry, Gentilly, Montrouge, Vanves and Issy. Paris had doubled in size, and now the octroi duties were collected at the Thiers Wall. Just as everyone feared. Just as politicians had promised never to do.

The famous caricaturists Honoré Daumier and Charles Vernier navigated the constraints of imperial censorship to join the public discussion on this territorial plundering. In one cartoon, Daumier depicts a poorly dressed, clog-wearing couple in front of their shack in the middle of a field. The caption says: 'Can you believe we're Parisians now?' While Vernier portrays Paris as an elegant lady wearing a crown made of fortifications, forcefully cleaning her dirty children, La Villette, Bercy and Belleville. In another cartoon, the same personification of the city pursues tiny protesting bourgeois carrying placards that read, 'Auteuil', 'Passy' and 'Boulogne'. She is about to capture them under her crinoline underskirt, on which the caricaturist has written 'octroi'. The wall had become a political and fiscal threshold more than a military one, the physical manifestation of an ogrish, treacherous Paris devouring all surrounding municipalities as it expanded.

Suburban mayors' bitterness lives on. In 1992, they were invited to the Pavillon de l'Arsenal – a municipal exhibition space dedicated to architecture and urban planning – for the vernissage of an exhibition curated by Jean-Louis Cohen and André Lortie dedicated to 'the thresholds of the city'. The urbane cocktail quickly turned sour when elected officials of the banlieue used that platform to collectively demand the restitution of the lands that had been annexed to the City of Paris by Napoleon III in 1859.

Within twenty years, the nature and identity of Paris had changed profoundly. Its surface area had doubled to include municipal towns with their own identities that had vehemently protested such integration. For the first time since the seventeenth century, Paris was bounded by a military infrastructure made of a continuous wall thirty-four kilometres long supported by sixteen detached forts spread across the suburbs. Prefect Haussmann was busy 'bludgeon[ing] the city into modernity', in David Harvey's words.[4] It was an enterprise widely understood by contemporaries and historians as an attempt to install anti-insurgency hardware into the city by way of urban planning. Parisians, especially the riotous working classes, were under siege, controlled by an autocratic power busy turning the capital city into a real estate El Dorado.

I came across a peculiar map from 1843 that vividly illustrates the ambiguity of this situation. Titled 'Map of the Paris Fortifications', the chart also displays the firing lines of all detached forts surrounding the city.

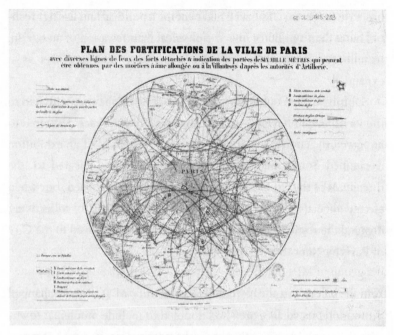

Map of Paris fortifications dated 1843 where the firing
range of each fort has been represented.

It is atypically composed of a round frame with Paris at its centre.
Drawn from all sixteen forts are circles with radii of 6,000 metres: the
cannons' reach. The circles representing the firing range are incomplete, and they do not extend to the countryside surrounding Paris.
Instead, it seems the forts' cannons are aimed at Paris. The map shows
that the city is almost entirely within firing range of the newly built
mortars, specifically all working-class neighbourhoods in the Old
Paris and the new, post-annexation city limits. Only the most affluent
neighbourhoods, the Louvre, Place de la Concorde and the yet-to-be-
annexed Batignolles cannot be reached by the cannons. The message,
intentional or not, is clear: Parisians are within firing range. This map
realises the fears Arago expressed in the 1830s of counterrevolutionary

infrastructure aimed more at restricting the people's civil liberties than fortifying the city against invasion. Twenty years after its completion, the military infrastructure enclosing Paris was about to be tested.

On 19 July 1870, France declared war on Prussia. By 2 September, France had capitulated. Two days later Napoleon III was stripped of his power, the empire was abolished and the Third Republic was soon proclaimed. Summoned by the president of parliament as a matter of urgency, MPs started debating the future of Napoleon III at 1 a.m. on 4 September. Frustrated by the lack of progress and pressured by a crowd of Parisians that had stormed the building, Republican MP Léon Gambetta exhorted the mob – 'To City Hall!' There, on behalf of a group of MPs that he led, Gambetta announced the new regime, from the balcony of the town hall, and the following call to arms was printed and posted all over town.

> The People preempted the Parliament that hesitated. To save the endangered Nation, they called for a Republic . . . The Republic is proclaimed . . . Citizens, watch over the City that has been entrusted to you; tomorrow you will be, together with the army, the Nation's avengers.

The people of Paris had once again set the country on a new political course.

The temporary government that had seized power did not accept Napoleon III's capitulation and vowed to continue the fight. On 17 September, the Prussian Army reached Paris and started the siege of the city. Paris resisted for more than three months before formally surrendering. In January an armistice was signed in the Hall of Mirrors, Palace of Versailles. The Thiers Wall had arguably slowed the progression of enemy forces – the siege of 1814, by comparison, had lasted only twenty-four hours – but it was no match against the shells of the Krupp cannons that had hit Paris without much difficulty, while the Prussian long-range weapons remained well beyond the firing lines of the detached forts.

On 1 March 1871, as per the conditions of the armistice, the Prussian Army entered Paris and set up a camp on Place de la Concorde. Tension was rife between, on the one hand, the people of Paris and the National Guard – a municipal military force made up of volunteers – and, on the other, the Prussian and French armies. Adolphe Thiers, who had once again become head of state *and* head of the government just a few weeks before, made a fatal error of judgement and tried to disarm the Parisians, by removing cannons placed on top of the Montmartre Hill. The move triggered a backlash from the city and its National Guard. The people of Paris were up in arms against 'Pipsqueak' Thiers, who, the same day, fled the capital city with his government to find refuge in Versailles. The Commune had started.

A formidable uprising, a revolutionary government that has left a durable mark on the history of socialism, the story of the Commune cannot be told in a nutshell. This socialist utopia built by the women and men of Paris would eventually be crushed by loyalist forces, known as the *versaillais*, during the 'Bloody Week' of May 1871. The same month, Karl Marx published a pamphlet in English celebrating the Commune: *The Civil War in France*. The uprising marked the apotheosis of a rebellious working-class city – after the revolutions of July 1789, July 1830 and February 1848 that all led to regime changes.

The Commune was not a bourgeois revolution; it was a socialist project imagined by the Parisian masses. It has a heavy legacy that interweaves culture, politics and the built environment, and it remains active and disputed to this day. In February 2021, in the run-up to the commemoration events planned for the 150th anniversary of the

Commune, the conservative opposition in the Council of Paris reiterated its hostility to any endeavour to 'glorify' the Commune of 1871, sparking a debate with the left and green coalition, headed by the socialist mayor Anne Hidalgo.

The Commune has also been analysed as being the result of the social segregation of Haussmann's *grand travaux*. Baron Haussmann's 'strategic embellishments' resulted in the exclusion of working classes from the historic city centre, and even from the city proper. In *The Emergence of Social Space*, the professor of comparative literature Kristin Ross writes that

> the workers' redescent into the centre of Paris [during the Commune] followed in part from the political significance of the city centre within a tradition of popular insurgency, and in part from their desire to reclaim the public space from which they had been expelled, to reoccupy streets that once were theirs.[5]

By destroying the oldest and poorest neighbourhoods of the city without necessarily offering compensation, Haussmann effectively displaced thousands of Parisians from their home districts, in the exterior arrondissements, in the banlieue and in a liminal place right outside the Thiers Wall: the Zone.

Earlier in this chapter, I described the architectural composition of the Thiers Wall. The fortifications, together with a 40-metre ditch, were completed on the outside by an easement 250 metres deep and about 34 kilometres long. In urban planning, an easement is a plot of land with a specific set of rules attached to it. In this case it was a military easement, imposing a *non-ædificandi* order: in theory, it was forbidden to erect any construction on that land.

Fortified French cities in the eighteenth and nineteenth centuries were traditionally surrounded by three rings of land under easement. On the first ring, construction was strictly prohibited so that a city's defenders could fire, without obstacle, at enemy troops besieging the town. On the second strip of land that extended a distance of half a kilometre, it was authorised only to build in wood and earth, and with the knowledge that the military authorities could decide to bring down any construction without compensation or advance warning in case of siege. The final ring of easement, which went up to a one-kilometre distance from the fortifications, forbade changing the landscape without explicit authorisation – any new ditch, hill, canal and so on needed to be approved by the army. In Paris, in acknowledgement of the city's existing urban density, only the first ring was implemented, and only partially. Indeed, a legal ambiguity had messed up the status of this area *non-ædificandi*. Paris had never been designated as a 'place of war', as the law required. And so, while the army considered the forbidden area to be under strict military rules, others did not.

The overwhelming presence of the fortifications in the landscape in conjunction with the Zone is best illustrated by a 1913 bird's-eye-view picture of the town of Issy-les-Moulineaux, southwest of Paris.

The photograph was shot from the top of the fortifications and looks at the suburbs. On the right-hand side, we see the redan fortifications that surround the city, the ditch and embankment that continue into the Zone. Covered with grass, they are free from any construction or even allotments. We see people strolling, including a woman in a long dress. She stands in the foreground and seems to look up at the photographer, who is probably hidden behind a large view camera.

The Zone by the town of Issy, in 1913.

Then there is the Zone: shacks and gardens and modest buildings that might house small factories. We can spot several water towers too. Further out, the proper suburbs commence with the town of Issy, where buildings gain a few storeys. Consider the intense fracture comprising a series of horizontally layered splits that the fortifications and the Zone constituted. From the 1840s until the 1930s, when the fortifications were decommissioned, this four-hundred-metre area marked the separation between the city of Paris and the banlieue.

Upset by Haussmann's grand plans and shellshocked by the Prussian invasion of 1870–1 and the subsequent Commune crushed by the bourgeois government of Adolphe Thiers, working-class Parisians had had a rough time since the erection of the Thiers Wall in the 1840s. Haussmann's projects were specifically aimed at reshaping the space of Paris to enable the bourgeoisie to reclaim an embellished city centre. The urbanist Louis Lazare writes in 1865 about the 'forced emigration of workers towards the outlying districts and the towns outside Paris,' but characterises this as a positive move for the well-being of the blue-collar workers of Paris, as the 'air is healthier and housing more affordable'.[6] Contemporary theoreticians of urbanism and architecture agreed with such views.[7] But Haussmann's ambitions were a far cry from Lazare's philanthropic interpretation. In an 1857 letter, for instance, the Baron wrote:

> I need everyone's help . . . to cut open these great strategic thoroughfares that will go from the centre to the outer limits of Paris, that will push back workers outside the city in order to spread them out and that will also enable us to pursue them and control them if needed.[8]

Haussmann's reshaping of Paris was an operation guided by 'order' and 'beauty': declutter the city, remove the insalubrious Old Paris to erect the tall, modern buildings of the future, turn the built environment from an enemy to an ally of law enforcement as it repressed rebellious Parisians and remove a population the authorities considered riotous, dirty and unfit to live in a modern city centre.

Paris and the surrounding banlieue were going through profound changes. Industrial activities were dislodged from the city centre and relocated to the newly annexed arrondissements of the northeast: the tenth, eleventh, eighteenth, nineteenth and twentieth, and beyond the Thiers Wall. The economy and culture of the banlieue quickly shifted from mostly agricultural activities in the 1860s to a dense industrial urban fabric by the end of the nineteenth century.[9] Workers lived close to their workplaces at the time – there were limited public transportation options, private cars were rare and the bicycle was a few

years away from becoming omnipresent on Paris's streets – and logically followed their jobs. Those who could stay faced inflated rents
and an increased cost of living. 'You have to understand', says a landlord to his tenant in an 1854 caricature by Chagot, 'that my house is
now on Rue de Rivoli and I have to increase your rent ten-fold'.[10]
Parisians had initially moved outside the Wall of the General Farm,
to avoid the high octroi. On average a Parisian paid eight times in
octroi what a *banlieusard* did.[11] With the 1860 annexation, 400,000
inhabitants of the suburbs became Parisians, and experienced a quick
impoverishment that led many to move further out into the suburbs.[12]
For businesses, it meant a steep increase in their costs – and the departure of some of their workforce.

Right outside the city walls, and cheaper than the banlieue, the
Zone was an attractive space to resettle. In the forbidden area mushroomed a liminal city, an alternative Paris. The Zone was outside the
Parisian octroi, and it was cheaper to live there because construction
was formally forbidden. Building one's home in the Zone was a risk;
the police or the military could raid and destroy it without warning.
A decision by the Council of State, one of France's supreme courts,
ruled on 24 July 1856 that the Zone was indeed under military juris-
diction and that any constructions there would have to be destroyed.
The decision remained largely unheeded.[13] Yet the threat remained.
A thorough history of the Zone remains unwritten, but historians
agree that shacks started popping up on the strip of land as soon as the
Thiers Wall was completed in the 1840s, and by 1880 it was quite
densely populated.

On weekends, Parisians of all classes strolled and picnicked outside
the fortifications. Writers and artists idealised this in-between space.
The 1865 naturalist novel *Germinie Lacerteux*, by the writers and

socialites Edmond and Jules de Goncourt, depicts the area beyond the fortifications as a place of leisure for the people of Paris. In 1887, the Dutch painter Vincent van Gogh moved to the northwestern suburb of Asnières and painted the fortifications by Porte de Clichy. Thirty years later, a young Edward Hopper created beautiful etchings of Parisians on the Zone, now in the collection of the MoMA in New York City. Cabarets, brothels, *bistro* and theatres have all set up their activities on the Zone, reinforcing the image of this restricted area as louche, dangerous. By the end of the nineteenth century, the Zone had become the archetypal Parisian *bas-fond*, a rough place. In 1908, a lawyer and social reformer named Flourens writes:

> The Zone has its inhabitants and its cabarets, usually dodgy ones: this is not the least of its inconveniences. The population in the vicinity is mainly composed of ragpickers, vagrants, and people of no faith of either sex living in great promiscuity, housed in shacks or even in caravans and old carriages, with no consideration for hygiene. These people do not own: they are tenants, more or less official, and often with no contracts whatsoever. Crimes of all kinds, theft, and robberies, are in this area more common than anywhere else; any police surveillance or searching of offenders is especially hard. And finally, these people's living conditions are dubious regarding salubrity. They form for the nearby towns and the outer districts of Paris unwholesome and dangerous neighbours, and an endless source of anxiety and complaints.[14]

Vagrants, Roma, immigrants, criminals, ragpickers. Back a century, we reconnect with the *biffins* of Porte Montmartre. In nineteenth- and early twentieth-century Paris, at a time when the citywide collection of garbage did not exist, rag-and-bone (wo)men were essential actors of what we would call today the 'circular economy'.

Often at night, a ragpicker went through the waste of the city, using a hook – hence the name 'moon anglers' – to rummage through the mounds of rubbish, and selected the materials and objects in which they saw some value: the ends of cigars reused to make cheap tobacco, pieces of wool reconstituted to make clothes, hair sold to hairdressers, rabbit skins, and animal bones that could be fashioned into knife handles and buttons or cooked to produce fertiliser, gelatine, or bone char.[15]

A ragpicker's home was also where they stored, took apart, dried, cooked, burned and transformed the items they gleaned. A place to hoard and where, eventually, the waste of the waste was abandoned to rot. At a time when social hygiene movements, together with a new organicist understanding of urbanism (large streets to disperse miasma and favour access to sunshine, open green spaces, in conjunction with moral postures such as teetotalism), became mainstream, ragpickers were stigmatised as transmitters of diseases, as vermin spreading vermin. In his 1885 book *Paris's Topography, Hygiene and Diseases*, Léon Colin writes that *chiffoniers'* dumps are for their neighbours a source of 'unbearable stench' because of 'the number of bones and rabbit skins still fresh' that will be left to dry. 'Located inside the city, where they keep masses of suspicious objects that could have been soiled by persons sick from contagious diseases. They are, furthermore, because of their constant back-and-forth journeys, agents spreading the diseases.'[16] He goes on to explain that the authorities were considering banning them from the city.

With Haussmann's grand plans, stigmatised communities of *chiffoniers* were pushed out from the central arrondissements and relocated to the outer limits of the city, and already on the Zone. They regrouped in *cités*, a word – not yet associated with 1960s modernist social housing – that described small and self-contained urban communities, relatively isolated from the rest of the urban fabric, and usually organised around one central street or courtyard, or a series of interconnected courtyards. Among the most famous of its time was the Cité Doré (literally, 'Golden City') in the thirteenth arrondissement. In 1854, Alexandre Privat d'Anglemont, a writer and archetypal Parisian *bohème*, described the Cité Doré:

> Further away than Japan, more unknown than Africa, in a district where nobody has ever been, there exists something incredible, incomparable, peculiar, horrendous, charming, dreadful, admirable. You have heard about the carbets of the Caribbean, the ajoupas of Maroons villages, the wigwams of the savages, of Arabs' tents: but nothing looks like that. It is even more extraordinary than what we can describe. Tartars' camps must be palaces in comparison. And yet, this thing that would make any central Parisian shiver, is in Paris.[17]

Note the racist images used by Privat d'Anglemont – despite being himself a Guadeloupe-born Afro-descendant who endured the racism of nineteenth-century Paris – who compares the *chiffoniers* and their dwellings to native architecture in remote lands of Africa and the Americas. Even if the rest of his chapter dedicated to the 'city of the ragpickers' is slightly more nuanced, we recognise here the figure of speech that became a classic device of the literature on cities: a metonymy between hygiene, class and race on the one hand, and the architecture where these stigmatised social groups live on the other. The people and their urban environment are concatenated in an inextricable relationship, slowly leading to a toxic understanding of urban planning where the removal of a population and the obliteration of their dwellings in the name of social hygiene would become one and the same thing.

The Zone was just that, a place where a population kicked out from the city proper had found solace, only to be stigmatised by the bourgeois elite of France. The Zone was the archetypal 'slum', a word so often used by the dominant classes to persecute subaltern populations in the name of hygiene and social progress that urban planners and architects should consider it taboo. They called it the 'black belt' of Paris – *la ceinture noire*.

The Zone had become the incoming area for all the populations that Paris has rejected, expelled, 'cleansed'. Ragpickers, workers, migrants, Roma. What Karl Marx and Friedrich Engels would call Paris's *lumpenproletariat* – *lumpen* incidentally meaning 'rags' or 'ragged' in German. By association with its occupants, the Zone became the civilisation's antonym: on the edges of the city of light stood its abyss, its dark forest, its dump, its no-man's land, its no-go Zone. The outcasts of Paris, such as the *chiffoniers*, were described as savages, barbarians and nomads that 'do not know where they come from' or where they belong.

Those in the Zone were the stereotypical Parisian 'scum': transient people in between jobs, 'landlord without land, tenant without rent'.[18] In a speech in front of the Paris City Council in 1864, Baron Haussmann justified the fact that Parisians were not allowed to elect their mayors, because they did not constitute a 'community' of citizens:

> Workers, by hundreds of thousands, swarm to Paris, seeking high wages, and save enough money to retire in their own country. Among those who stay . . . many, in too big numbers, tossed around from workshop to workshop, hostel to hostel, their only household being public places, their only relatives are charitable organisations, where they seek help in their hardship, are genuine nomads at the heart of the Parisian Society, totally deprived of any municipal sentiment.[19]

The Zone is miscellaneous. It is a myth, an element of Parisian lore. For the anthropologist Jérôme Beauchez, the Zone was a physical space of course, but it remains an idea. The Zone and its *zonards*, an argotic negative term to describe those who doss around, might not exist in space, but their spirits endure – they are the punks of the 1990s, the youth of the banlieue today. I have depicted with my own words and those of others the fear and the hatred that the Zone and its inhabitants inspired in the dominant classes. I have shown how the Zone crystallised a discourse on urban planning that conflated people with their environment. I have started telling you how the crafting of a space and a category, the Zone and its logical continuation, the banlieue, constituted the invention of an alterity for the bourgeois of Paris, an Other, a subaltern, a savage.

Let's end this chapter with the photographs of Eugène Atget, who candidly and tenderly captured the lives of the *chiffoniers* in the Zone, a far cry from the miserabilist, sensationalist or paternalist depictions of this space at the time. From 1897 until his death in 1927, Atget, a former actor who turned to photography after a disease that affected his vocal cords, photographed Paris, its architecture, its heritage and – more rarely – its people. When he did represent individuals, he focused on those who worked and lived on the streets of the city. Atget's work is well known to us because in the last years of his life, the surrealist movement, especially Man Ray and a young Berenice Abbott, praised Atget's views of Paris and made sure his photographs made their way to public collections, where they remain accessible today.

In *The Work of Art in the Age of Mechanical Reproduction*, Walter Benjamin describes Atget's work as if they were images of a crime scene: 'With Atget, photographs become standard evidence for historical occurrences, and acquire a hidden political significance.'[20] The series of pictures Atget shot of the *zoniers* is a precious representation of the area in the 1910s. It is touching to note Atget named the series after the inhabitants, the *zoniers*, instead of the toponym, the Zone. He photographs the shacks made of cob and plaster, surrounded by neat little gardens to grow vegetables.

The houses are built from materials gleaned in Paris; here is a flat probably recycled from a café, bearing a faded mention of a *'téléphone'*: the family sits for Atget. Only the woman has managed to stand still during the long exposure, and her features are clearly captured.[21] In another, a makeshift house has been adorned with a strange collection of dolls, stuffed birds and two rocking sheep that watch over from the roof. Plants have been invited to ascend the facade by way of strings going from the flowerpot to the slate.[22]

Poterne des Peupliers, in 1913. From series 'Les Zoniers', by Eugène Atget.

Porte de Montreuil, in 1912. From series 'Les Zoniers', by Eugène Atget.

And here, next to the Roma's caravans there is an ice cream cart: *vaniglia* and *ciocolat*, ten cents, lemonade, ten cents, *coco* – a home-made beverage of liquorice macerated in a lemony water – five cents.[23] The spelling of the ice cream flavours is a testimony of the immigrant population freshly arrived from Italy that settled in the Zone, bring-ing delicious recipes of *gelati* for the hot summer days spent frolick-ing on the slopes of the fortifications.

Atget's photographs depict decent working-class people living in dire conditions. Impoverished Parisians, migrants from rural France or from abroad and travellers have sought in the Zone a place that they can afford, even if it comes with the daily threat of being kicked out by the police or the military. Yet the living conditions represented in the photographs are obviously precarious, inadequate. We see fragile makeshift houses lacking water access, electricity, gas, mains drainage, pavement or macadam. At the turn of the twentieth century, the Zone was the ultimate slum. Together with its habitants, the Zone had a target on its back.

2
Green Belt: Greenwashing, Whitewashing

The tiny dog lifts its right back paw and pees on the streetlamp. It is a typical Parisian lamppost, made of casted metal painted in dark forest green, adorned with sculpted ivy that climbs all the way up where it is topped with a light bulb inside a lantern. A heritage of nineteenth-century Paris, with a touch of the Art Nouveau fascination for curvaceous plants and flowers. On an old wall half-covered with vegetation, where the friable mortar has progressively revealed the irregular hand-cut stones that have turned black over the centuries, a child has written *mon oncle* in awkward cursive writing using white chalk.

The dachshund, now relieved, pursues its jog in the streets of Paris. It roams as elegantly and proudly as its tiny stature and short legs allow, weighed down by a dog coat made of red tartan. The cheeky, pricy-looking animal explores the city in the company of a bunch of playful street dogs, bantering and eating food out of humans' bins – masterfully removing the lids with a single paw kick – and yesterday's market's leftovers. It is a wet, grey early morning.

Shop windows with their traditional wooden signs hanging from above the door are shut and the streets are empty, except for a ragpicker whose horse-drawn cart is full of the fabrics, objects and materials he gleaned overnight. The man is old, the last of a generation, the last of a dying trade. He moves slowly and calmly, securing the ware with ropes while his horse awaits patiently, used to a lifetime spent along-side stray dogs in the picturesque streets of charming, run-down Paris in the morning. The sound of jingle bells and the knocking of hoofs on the pavement of Paris announces the cart's departure, followed by the joyful barking of a cortege of enthusiastic pups.

The ragpicker continues his journey into the modern city, with newly built, pristine high-rise housing in the background. A collapsed wall overgrown with weeds, made of stone and red brick, with a dislodged cast-iron fence and tumbling shutters – over which jumps the dachshund – acts as the boundary between Old and New Paris. In the latter, no bins to eat from, but neatly macadamed streets with arrows and traffic signs to tell you where to go and how to behave, slender, austere neon-lit streetlamps and carefully cut shrubberies, with no room for nature's exuberance. The opening scene of Jacques Tati's classic *My Uncle* finishes on the classy tartan-donned dog rejoining the posh, neatly designed, slightly boring detached house of its owners, Monsieur and Madame Arpel.

Tati's movie was made in 1958, at a time of intense change in Paris's urban fabric – from reconstruction to 'slum-clearance', road building to New Towns. It is a masterful take on the relation between modernism and nature in urban space: where the enticing aesthetics of the electric city are all about rules, self-control and the hierarchy of social classes dominated by the technologies of capitalism, while Old Paris is a dirty but enticing and playful space where the street sweeper talks more than he works and gets paid an early afternoon glass of wine by the bourgeois he argued with a minute before. The plants of Old Paris are unruly and omnipresent – growing in the cracks of the pavement, out of people's balconies, and on the mossed slanted roofs, while the vegetation of New Paris is circumscribed to specifically designed spaces shaped by secateurs, disciplined by lawnmowers, policed by herbicides.

Between the Old and the New Paris is the Zone. Where grass roams loose, children play hide-and-seek before breaking with a beignet topped with jam and lovers come frolicking. The Zone is unpoliced, away from the city and its norms, an in-between space, fractious, a free space.

The planning of Paris and its suburbs is often dominated by what the environmental sociologist Hillary Angelo has called the 'green-as-good' logic – the assumption that anything 'green' is inherently positive.[1] But greening has been used across history as a vehicle to separate Paris from its peripheries and to exclude its subaltern populations: *banlieusards*, immigrants, working classes, Roma, Jews. This goes all the way back to post-Haussmann Paris and the debates over the removal of 'Monsieur Thiers's Great Wall of China', as well as the creation of a green belt around early twentieth-century Paris. To understand today's Paris, we also need to understand the heritage of 'green Vichy', the role of landscape design in relation to infrastructure building in the 1930s in Nazi Germany and collaborating France, its connection to the present-day ring road and to its future as a 'new green belt'.

In 1882, Member of Parliament Martin Nadaud proposed the first bill to remove the fortification walls of Paris. In his speech, he explained that 'the great city [of Paris] choked in its straitjacket', and that to delay its removal would be to sacrifice the future of the city's 'valiant and hard-working people'.[2]

For many, the defeat of 1870 had revealed the irrelevance of the Thiers Wall, and Nadaud's call for its removal was well timed. But it would take over half a century to see its final demise. In the way stood a variety of stakeholders that tried to claim ownership of the future of the fortifications and the surrounding Zone. The debate involved politicians, financiers, urban planners, architects and the army, as well as lawyers, doctors, intellectuals and artists. It also included, to a lesser extent, Parisians, *banlieusards* and *zoniers*.

The total surface area of 1,200 hectares represented a massive land stock for Paris, a city of 8,000 hectares in 1870. It was a tantalising prospect for developers and a once-in-a-century opportunity for urbanists and aediles. The debate on the removal of the fortifications also took place at a time of rapid population growth and fast urban expansion. The population of Paris had grown from half a million souls in 1801 to 2 million in 1876, and hit 2.7 million people in 1901 before reaching its peak in 1921 at 2.9 million. Land was scarce, housing was dire and often in a poor state, overcrowding was omnipresent – especially for workers. What was at stake was the future of Paris as well as of France, the health of the Parisians and the role of the built environment in shaping their morality, their attitudes, their social values and ultimately their politics. And if not that, it could be, at least, a way of securing their docility.

The sprawling city also urgently needed to build its transport infrastructure for the decades to come. Walking, cycling, horse-drawn carts, engine-powered automobiles, subterranean railways and even air travel – all these solutions were envisioned, tested, discussed and drawn up by engineers, architects, novelists, artists. The urban real estate occupied by the fortifications was the perfect space to project all these dreams onto: it could be turned into hundreds of thousands of homes for Parisians – social housing for the *ouvriers* or luxurious condominiums for the wealthy; it was a virgin land to host transport infrastructure to surround the capital city with a

much-needed orbital network; it could also be turned into a gigantic
annular park, a vital amenity for a city that had so few green spaces to
offer its population.

As the architectural historians Jean-Louis Cohen and André Lortie
explain, London was the inspiration for Nadaud and intellectual elites
at the time. Many politicians, urbanists and architects had visited the
rival city. Socialists in exile or those simply seeking a more liberal
regime – such as Karl Marx, Friedrich Engels, Élisée Reclus – had
found a haven in Victoria's capital. The imperial city was also the
home of Louis-Napoléon Bonaparte, future Napoleon III, before his
successful comeback and election as president in 1848, and once again
after his 1870 disgrace, until his death three years later. French elites
across the political spectrum had a good understanding of London's
urbanism and its iconic projects: Regent Street (completed in 1825),
the Great Exhibition of 1851, Joseph Bazalgette's sewerage system
built throughout the 1860s and 1870s, the Underground, whose initial
Metropolitan Line opened in 1863, railway stations such as Euston
(1837), Paddington (1838), Waterloo (1848), St. Pancras (1868) and
so on.

Britain was also praised in French circles for its strategy to declutter Central London districts. That is to say, the obliteration of 'slums'
such as St. Giles, present-day Holborn, in the 1830s and the development of the suburbs: detached and semidetached houses served by a
fast-growing network of trains, boosted by the Cheap Train Act of
1883, which allowed a wider array of Londoners to live further away
from their workplaces and commute.[3] The creation of 'open spaces'
for Londoners of all classes, including new royal parks such as
Regent's Park (1835), but mostly new council parks like Victoria Park
(1845), Battersea Park (1858) and Alexandra Park (1863), was especially praised by the French.

But while London was a model that many thinkers, socialists and anarchists especially looked up to, it was also a site of exploitation of the poorest. The city was the expression of the *malady* of urbanisation, equalled to a monster 'expanding day by day and almost hour by hour, engulfing year by year fresh colonies of immigrants, and running out their suckers, like giant octopuses, into the surrounding country', wrote the anarchist and geographer extraordinaire Élisée Reclus, in English, for London's *Contemporary Review* in 1895.[4]

Following Nadaud's initial attempt, several bills and motions pushed for the removal of the fortifications. But the debate on what might replace them was far from settled. First, the army had then not completely renounced fortifying the capital city. Despite the 1870 defeat, the strategists did not immediately see the wall as obsolete. In 1874, a new series of forts was voted on and built further away from the city centre. Most of them still exist today, removed from active service – in Aubervilliers, Charenton, Ivry and so on. That changed, though, in the 1880s, with the invention of artillery shells filled with picric acid, or melinite, that could blow traditional brick-laid fortification. Despite this, in the discussion on the removal of the Thiers Wall, the army sought to sell the land at a good price to fund the construction of a *new* continuous wall built at a greater distance. In 1904 the defence minister finally gave in and renounced building this new wall around the capital.

At the same time, Paris was dealing with strong centripetal forces. Haussmann had decreased housing density in Central Paris and pushed outwards the most disrupting industries and trades, relocating them to the suburbs. The cost of living in the city proper was high, and the influx of migrants (from other parts of France and abroad) was constant and growing. The seventy-eight suburban municipalities in the Seine *département* – an administrative entity that was

disbanded in the 1960s and that roughly matches today's Greater
Paris Metropolitan government – were governed by as many mayors
and did not necessarily have what we would today call an urban planning policy.

To a large extent, the contrast between the urban fabric of Paris
and the banlieue has remained to this day. Twentieth-century urban
planning had a go at modifying, removing, decluttering, then
re-densifying the tissue of the Greater Paris. But walk down the Rue
de Paris and its adjacent streets in Montreuil – a suburban town so
closely connected to Paris it is nicknamed the 'twenty-first arrondissement' – and you will see a grand neo-Haussmannian building
standing on its own at number 196, immediately followed by a two-
storey that probably housed workshops until recently, then a 1980s
hotel. And at number 188, a single-family house that is now a furniture shop selling bespoke Moroccan living rooms. Then explore the
side street, and you will find a neo-rural urban fabric comprising
modest houses, often self-built by working-class Parisians and
banlieusards in the early twentieth century – that now sell for millions
– next to modernist HLM of unequal architectural quality.

The suburbs of Paris grew 'organically', without much energy
spent trying to control and organise this growth. Authorities focused
their efforts on Paris proper, the City of Light, the 'Queen of Beauty'
– not only because it was politically and culturally significant, but
also because it represented an enormous stash of gold.

What were the political and financial contexts behind the debate on
what to do with the walls? The fortifications of Paris and the surrounding Zone represented a lot of land and therefore a lot of money. When
the army renounced its project to build a new wall further away from
the city centre, which required selling the current fortifications at the

highest possible price, the pressure on the negotiations was reduced. The state did not have any reason to maintain costly infrastructure and to sit on land at the heart of one of Europe's booming cities that could be put to better use. Nevertheless, the City of Paris and the state had to agree on a good price. And like any developers, the city needed a 'business plan': how would they develop the area? How much income did they expect from this operation? And with those elements in mind, how much were they ready to pay for it?

The idea to use some, if not all, of that land to build an ambitious green space emerged early. The lawyer and writer Ernest Hamel proposed in 1885 to plant trees on the Zone and turn this 'desert' into an 'oasis'. At the same time, the Department for Public Works at Paris City Hall led by Adolphe Alphand proposed a design for the space of the fortifications and the area *non-ædificandi*. The engineer Alphand, who served as head of the department for *promenades et plantations* under Baron Haussmann and who replaced him after the fall of the Second Empire, proposed to secure a *réservoir d'air* around Paris. He was inspired by the examples of Frankfurt and especially Vienna's Ringstrasse.

Alphand and his administration proposed a large thoroughfare seventy-four metres wide on Paris's side – that included a light barrier to collect the octroi tax – and, in place of the fortifications, housing blocks sixty-five to eighty-five metres wide. In the project, the Zone was not directly considered, except that any value added to the *zoniers'* properties was captured by way of a special tax.

For Jean-Louis Cohen and André Lortie, who have analysed in-depth the long debates on the fortifications in their book *Des fortifs au périf*, this first project was not only about replacing the fortifications with new homes but also about reintroducing the available land to the market. Cohen and Lortie also note that the neo-Haussmannian approach advocated by Alphand was already passé by the time it was published. And yet, against all odds, it would eventually prevail several decades later.

But not so fast. The negotiations between the city and the state fell through several times and the Alphand project was shelved. Alphand himself, the great heir to Baron Haussmann, died in 1891, a few months after his mentor. At the dawn of a new century, the future of the fortifications was yet to be decided, when a new generation of urbanists and architects arrived with innovative ideas for Paris and its newly conceptualised metropolitan area.

In 1902, a new design guideline written by the city architect Louis Bonnier loosened the strict codes regarding building heights and projections onto the streets. Designers and planners had got bored with the rigid heritage of Haussmann as they became infatuated with Art Nouveau and its abundance of organic curves inspired by trees and flora. A new wave of architects reignited the debate on the foremost aesthetic and social issue of its time: the removal of the fortifications and the future of Paris. A visionary architect, Eugène Hénard, by that time in his fifties, played a significant role in imagining a future for the Thiers Wall. His influence on the new discipline of urban planning in France, as well as abroad in the United Kingdom and Germany, was significant and would have direct influence on the work of preeminent architects – Le Corbusier, for instance – and twentieth-century urban planning at large.

Hénard was actively involved in an organisation created in 1894, misleadingly named Musée Social. Much more than a museum, the Musée Social was a charity that brought together politicians, public intellectuals, architects and scientists, and that sat at the crossroad of a think tank (to use an anachronic term), a lobby group and a private club. Presided over by Jules Siegfried, a politician who had passed the first law to enable the emergence of social housing that same year 1894, the Musée Social was bankrolled by Count Aldebert Pineton de Chambrun, a direct descendent of Marquis de Lafayette who had married into the wealthy family owning the Baccarat crystal manufacturer.

The Musée Social was the home of the French social hygiene movement with its philosophy that combined physical bodies, morality and the built environment in a novel understanding of policy and science, significantly relying on 'quantitative' data and statistics. In 1908, it created a research group, the Urban and Rural Hygiene Section, that initially dedicated much of its energy to influencing the debate on the fortifications of Paris, with Hénard as its main voice.

From 1903 until 1909, Hénard published a series of papers in the periodical *L'Architecture* titled 'Studies on Architecture and the Transformation of Paris'. He envisioned the city of the twentieth century, which included installing helipads on top of Haussmannian buildings, more than twenty years before the first successful helicopter flight, and using the Champs de Mars in front of the Eiffel Tower, turned into control tower, as a landing strip for airships. Less spectacular, and yet just as revolutionary, was Hénard's research on the challenges of urban traffic and his invention of the roundabout.

At the same time, he had made several proposals for the fortifications: the first was a design strategy for a new boulevard around Paris that he called the *boulevard à redans*, a 'redan' being an arrow-shaped embankment forming part of a fortification. Inspired by the vocabulary of defence, ironically, Hénard had developed a system of housing built along a jagged edge in order to allow more light and air to come in, and break the monotony of Haussmann's boulevards.

He also wrote extensively on green open spaces, comparing Paris – unfavourably – to London. To lobby future councillors in favour of Hénard's project, the Musée Social produced in 1908 a map that roughly located twelve new, large parks on the edges of Paris, that candidates for the municipal council could sign to demonstrate their pledge to defend the project if elected. And in April 1909, the Musée Social put together a detailed proposal for the future of the fortifications, which Siegfried presented to the minister of the interior, the prefect and the head of the municipal council. The plan proposed building nine parks and thirteen playgrounds not only on the space of the fortifications but also on that of the Zone.

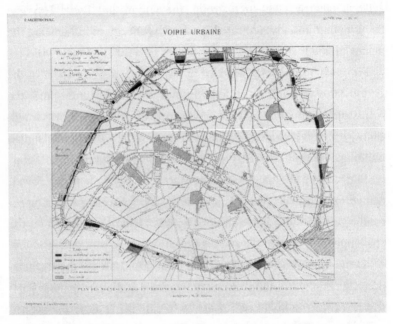

Masterplan by Eugène Hénard for the edges of Paris, published in 1909.

To avoid speculation, said Hénard, all owners should be expropriated before the removal of the fortifications and the cancellation of the military easement. Together, the parks and playgrounds would occupy about 168 hectares, with half on the fortifications and half in the Zone, increasing the surface area of green spaces in Paris by 60 per cent. The fortifications were to be replaced by a simple fence to collect the octroi. The rest of the space of the fortifications was to be sold to erect buildings. The whole operation could generate a profit of 70 million francs, which would contribute to purchasing the land from the state.[5]

Opposed to Hénard and the Musée Social was a conservative councillor named Louis Dausset. At the time the budget recorder in the Municipal Council of Paris, Dausset was an ambitious and influential local politician. Nationalist, reactionary, racist and anti-Semitic, Dausset made a name for himself by being fiercely anti-Dreyfus, vying against the French artillery officer of Jewish origin, wrongly sentenced to the penal colony for treason in 1894. Dausset was also the secretary general for the French Homeland League created in 1898 to oppose the Human Rights League founded the same year. The former brought together leading right-wing artists, scientists and intellectuals; the latter was a group of intellectual and social elites striving to rehabilitate Dreyfus and defend human rights.

Dausset also introduced aspects of social hygiene into city planning. The emergence of social hygiene in the second half of the nineteenth century coincided with the invention of racial theory and the development of industrial-era colonialism. Proponents of social hygiene connected the built environment not only to issues of morality, social behaviour and disease prevention, but also to questions of ancestry, race, bloodline and religion.

Today, it is a truism to say any grand urban planning design is inherently a social and political project. Arguably this perspective was even stronger and more violent at the turn of the twentieth century, a time of fast-paced socio-economic changes in European societies, when colonial empires were expanding while socialist revolts sprang up across the continent and a world war loomed. Removing a 'slum', building new houses and tracing a new road were not only technical or design issues but also social, political, racial and even civilisational ones. Louis Dausset's reactionary racism was central to his proposals for Paris.

On the surface, the Dausset proposal was even more radical than Hénard's. First, it required that all the land of the fortifications and the Zone be sold to the City of Paris by the state. Previous projects, including the Musée Social's, did not specifically demand that the whole Zone be treated in one single transaction. In Dausset's project, the fortifications were to be removed – and, on that aspect, all parties agreed. Then, the freed land of the fortifications would be sold off to public and private developers, to build thousands of homes. With the profits from the sales, the city would expropriate the whole of the Zone and expel the *zoniers* to turn the area into a 33-kilometre-long, 250-metre-wide green belt around Paris.

From a distance, Dausset's idea seems appealing – then and now. More homes for Parisians on the land of the fortifications, and a tree-lined green belt between Paris and the banlieue. But Hénard's rebuttal of the Dausset project in the columns of *L'Architecture* in 1909 shed light on the councillor's ambition. First, Hénard challenged the metaphors used by the proponents of Dausset's project, which presented this uninterrupted annular park as a *belt of pure air* while Dausset wrote in his report that 'the fortifications and the Zone constitute the only reserve where the air that the Parisian population breathes is constantly renewed'. This metaphor, also used by Alphand, has become a cliché, argued Hénard. The long park imagined by Dausset and his supporters would, in reality, be a sad-looking, hard-to-police stretch of land crisscrossed with roads on which 'automobiles would stir some noxious cloud'.[6]

Yet the true driver of Hénard's argument was yet to be revealed: real estate. The complex landscape of stakeholders and their intermingled vested interests has been described in detail by the historian Marie Charvet.[7] One key player was the syndicate for Parisian landlords. In January 1909, the syndicate created the League for Open Spaces to lobby in favour of Dausset's design. Hénard noted in his article that the secretary of the League and the secretary of the syndicate were the same individual. Parisian landlords were worried that if the whole Zone was built up, the price of properties in Paris would significantly decrease, while the landlords in the suburbs would get much richer. By retaining the easement on the Zone to prevent any new construction, argued the landlords and their supporters, it cut short any kind of speculation. And Hénard joked: 'Why not go even further and to prevent any decrease in the price of rents (sadly, not much probably), we could forbid any construction within a ten-kilometre radius from the fortifications. That, at least would be efficient.'[8]

What Dausset and his supporters aimed to create was not just a grand bucolic annular park surrounding the city, designed with the health and pleasure of inhabitants on both sides in mind, but a green *buffer* between Paris and its suburbs. This buffer had indeed a social and hygienic role, and it received support from many different stakeholders across the social and political spectrum. But this buffer was an instrumentalisation of greening for financial gain because it was designed to constrain permanently the growth of Paris and, in doing so, increase property values, enabling Parisian landlords to maintain high rents.

The Dausset project created a separation 'that would always prevent any contact between the old and the future Paris' wrote Hénard, offering a rare metropolitan reading of the space between Paris and its suburbs.[9] Dausset, with the support of landlords, proposed two concentric rings, 'one of stone, and one of greenery' to make the edges of Paris impermeable.[10] In contrast, Hénard's project was conceived as establishing a *suture* between the city proper and the banlieue. Along the fortifications and the Zone, Hénard proposed a series of diverse urban designs, which included his iconic parks, as well as connecting thoroughfares and new neighbourhoods.

In 1912, after more than thirty years of negotiation, the City of Paris, the state and the army reached an agreement and chose the Dausset proposal. It was enacted by two conventions signed on 16 and 30 December 1912. An already slow administrative process was put on hold by World War I, and it was only in 1919 that the conventions were turned into a law. Article 2 stipulated that the military easement for the Zone would be maintained in the form of an easement 'in the interest of hygiene and public health' and the works to remove the fortification started almost immediately on 30 April 1919.

Demolition of the fortifications by Porte d'Auteuil in 1920.

One century on, we can understand how discerning Hénard's critique of the Dausset project was. The divide between Paris and its suburbs was profoundly shaped by the landlords' green buffer, tinted with contempt for the *banlieusards*. Meanwhile, the Hénard project created very different conditions on which to build the future of metropolitan Paris. Historians have shown how many urbanists, architects and designers held conflicting views on the Dausset project, which fooled them by proposing a large open green space around Paris. Many did not have the sagacity to perceive the exclusionary social project hidden by the trees.

On 28 June 1919, in the Hall of Mirrors of the Palace of Versailles – to the west of Paris – the nations that fought one of the deadliest conflicts in global history finally settled on their respective punishments and retributions. A few months prior, the French parliament had passed two laws of major importance to the history of French urban planning. Established in March 1919, the Cornudet law made it mandatory that municipalities of 10,000 inhabitants or more produce an urban plan to organise their growth. And in April 1919, the decommissioning of the Thiers Wall was finally approved. Four decades had gone between the first bill that proposed taking down the fortifications in 1882 and the law that enacted their removal.

It took another decade to deconstruct the wall and several more to clear the Zone. If the Dausset project was eventually chosen for Paris, both laws marked the achievements of the Musée Social and the social hygiene movement that had started to gain momentum in the 1880s. A year after the Town Planning Conference, held in London in 1910, considered the first global meeting of its kind, the Société française des urbanistes was created, with Eugène Hénard at its head. The French Society for Urban Planners was so strongly connected to the

Musée Social that it was housed in the same mansion, on 5 Rue Las Cases in the seventh arrondissement, where the Musée Social is still based today. The social hygiene philosophy was therefore at the core of the French school of urban planning.

Social hygiene had its intellectual roots in political utopianism like Saint-Simonianism – an early nineteenth-century movement named after the Count of Saint-Simon, who correlated technological progress to humanity's happiness – but also found inspiration in international exemplars like Ebenezer Howard's Garden Cities in England. While its ambitions and vocabulary morphed after World War II, social hygiene arguably remained the primary guiding principle of French urbanism throughout the twentieth century and even to this day. For instance, in 2003, an ambitious programme for urban renewal, named Plan Borloo after the minister for urban affairs who led it, focused on the neighbourhoods that concentrated 'social, economic and urban issues' by targeting their built environment, mostly by retrofitting, deconstructing and building new housing.[11]

There were many – often intersecting – understandings of the principles of social hygiene. The tensions between the different political projects that used social hygiene as their catalyst in the interwar period are fundamental to study, not only for their impact on the relationship between Paris and banlieue but more largely for their influence on French planning thought in the century that followed.

At the turn of the twentieth century, the lexicon of architecture and urbanism was already filled with metaphors which characterised the city and its parts as a body with organs. Many of these images are commonplace today: a road is an *artery* that can get *clogged*, for instance. Large parks are a city's *lungs*. A lively neighbourhood is the *beating heart* of the town, and so on. The city, also, was compared to a sick body that needed healing. This understanding was then connected to tools like mapping and statistics, the first era of 'big data'. For instance, following a 1902 law on public health and hygiene in cities, Parisian authorities started to map out hotspots of socially stigmatised diseases like tuberculosis.[12] By associating a rate of death by tuberculosis higher than the Parisian average with specific 'blocks' – which French planning jargon calls *îlots*, literally 'islets', contributing to the perception that they are insulated from the rest of the urban tissue – planners and statisticians could point out a correlation between a disease, a category of population and the architecture they lived in.

Yet, like any technology, cartography and statistics can be the vehicle of moral and cultural prejudices. And when a correlation was identified (for instance, between a high death rate and a specific block) what remained was establishing a causality – a dangerous game at a time when urban planning was connected to violent political trends.

Charles Darwin's book *On the Origin of Species* (whose complete title is *On the Origin of Species by Means of Natural Selection, or the Preservation of Favoured Races in the Struggle for Life*), published in 1859 and translated into French in 1862, was read alongside the racist and 'scientific' book, by Arthur de Gobineau, *An Essay on the Inequality of the Human Races*, published in 1852. In this bestseller and early example of pseudoscientific racialism, Gobineau argues that there are three major racial groups – black, yellow and white – and that the white race is above the other races and that within the white race, the Aryan is superior. Various taxonomies of plants, animals and peoples also emerged that developed scientific or pseudoscientific theories to classify, rank and explain why some species survive, dominate, collapse and colonise.

The social hygiene movement was logically connected to these profound and extremely diverse intellectual trends. These discourses inspired visions for utopian humanist cities where people of all religions, ethnic origins and genders would live equally and happily, but it also fuelled a racialised understanding of the city and its maladies. Sadly, the latter gained so much strength that it became arguably the dominant discourse among French elites in the interwar period, a time of acute xenophobia, racism and anti-Semitism.

The infamous debate that took place on 2 December 1920 in the French Senate offers an illustration of how mainstream this approach had become. The subject was the measures that the government intended to take to deport unemployed foreigners living in French cities. The discussion in the upper house of the French parliament took place at a time when Paris was dealing with the outbreak of a mysterious epidemic nicknamed 'disease no. 9'. The code name given by health authorities was specifically designed to hide the truth: the city was facing its first significant outbreak of bubonic plague since the seventeenth century.

According to epidemiologists and historians, the controlled epidemic that eventually killed thirty-four broke out in May 1920 and had probably been dormant since 1917, when contaminated rats escaped an English boat carrying coal and other goods.[13] Later named the 'plague of the ragpickers', because many cases happened in the Zone among the *chiffoniers*, the epidemic eventually turned into a channel for anti-Semitism. During this debate, Senator Gaudin de Villaine denounced in his parliamentary speech the 'Oriental Jews that bring many diseases' and that are a 'threat' to Paris's 'health' as they 'creep in' and take over whole streets – 'hence the unbearable housing crisis for French working classes, French workers have to disappear and go live in the banlieue'.[14] Then a familiar character, freshly elected to represent Paris, welcomed the 'very interesting' speech by Gaudin de la Villaine before proposing his own insights.

Senator Louis Dausset described the 'repugnant scene' of Jewish households. These foreigners, he explained,

> carry not only the poison of revolution but also pernicious insects. They do not only compromise the moral health, but also the physical health of the population . . . Let us disinfect the spaces [they live in] . . . The eternal cause of contamination, I refer here to slums. This is precisely where we need to wage war.

The French expression used by Dausset literally called to 'carry the sword and the fire' onto the slums of Paris. He then concluded his address by asking the French government 'to help [the city] tackle this important issue intimately linked to the future of the race'. The minutes describe the reception of the speech: 'Loud applause, as he walks back to his seat, the orator is congratulated by his colleagues.'

By the mid-1930s, the fortifications had been entirely removed and the large-scale programme of housing designed to come in their place – which I will discuss in the next chapter – was by and large completed. But the Zone remained. A new law dated 10 April 1930 brought several significant amendments to the law of 1919 and created a new timeline: instead of thirty-eight years, the City of Paris now had fifteen years, starting in 1931, to acquire all properties of the Zone – which meant up until 31 December 1945. Yet for all those who lived on the Zone before 1919, the City of Paris had to offer a lease of twenty-five years to the *zoniers* whose property it purchased. In theory, this meant the Zone could be lawfully occupied until 31 December 1970. And so, the expropriation of the *zoniers* and the clearing of the Zone unfolded very, very slowly.

Meanwhile, new ideologies of urban planning and architecture emerged, together with a new technology that would define our modern relationship to space: the automobile. We immediately associate the landscape of cars with concrete and mineral, instead of greenery. This view is a far cry from the way road design was conceptualised in the 1930s, when the technology of motorways was imagined and the first projects built. Even when we look at the postwar renders – those programmes that obliterated our old city centres to create large concrete plazas and wide thoroughfares – we find they are full of trees and grass and bushes. As the architect and theoretician Éric Alonzo has shown, the design of the road is intimately linked to that of gardens.[15] To understand the urban design project for the green belt of Paris that emerged in the 1940s, and eventually became the Périphérique, we have to shift our focus and look at the country that inspired French engineers, architects and planners at the time: (Nazi) Germany.

The Battle of France started on 10 May 1940 and finished quickly. By June, most of the French and Allied forces were crushed. While Charles de Gaulle made an appeal from BBC's London studios on 18 June, denouncing the legitimacy of the capitulating government and calling for the French people to resist, the French State signed the armistice on 22 June. On 10 July 1940, the parliament, now based in the spa and resort town of Vichy, voted to entrust 'full powers' to Philippe Pétain, an eighty-four-year-old marshal, World War I 'hero' and statesman. In doing so, the parliament effectively dissolved the Third Republic, and democracy with it. Officially, the top half of the country was under German rule, while the rest of France – the so-called Free Zone – was governed by the Vichy regime in close collaboration with the Third Reich.

It is obvious to say 1940–4 were years of great upheaval and immense violence. But far from being solely a moment of war-dominated chaos, they were also a time of intense reform in France, especially when it came to urban planning and architecture. At the outset, the Vichy regime was perceived by some French elites as an opportunity to fix the issues that a sluggish Third Republic could not address, bogged down as it was by a cumbersome parliamentary regime. The same explanations for the defeat of 1870 were applied to that of 1940: a French 'backwardness', a weak state, an ageing elite and a lack of innovation.

The cancellation of democracy offered the 'opportunity' to develop a rational, scientific management that allowed swift and in-depth reform. Modernist architecture and urban planning, which had great ambitions to change people's lives by razing entire city blocks and replacing them with architecture suited for a 'new man', matched perfectly the technocratic and, to a certain extent, the fascist agenda of Pétain's France. Le Corbusier understood this well enough and knocked unsuccessfully yet insistently on dictators' doors – specifically, Mussolini's, Pétain's and Stalin's. Hitler's less so. He never managed to get any major commissions from them, however.[16] Perhaps luckily.

For many architects, planners and landscape designers, the Vichy regime was the perfect setting to engage with the complex entanglements between race, public health and the built environment – housing, as well as road infrastructure, parks and gardens. The landscape scholar Dorothée Imbert explains how French landscape designers embraced the *révolution nationale*, the name of Vichy's ideology, as they moved on from designing gardens for private clients to working on reconstruction projects – sports grounds and immense parks.[17] Pétain's ideology was grounded in an idealised rurality. In his speech broadcasted on the radio on 25 June 1940, in which he explained the conditions of the armistice to the French people, Pétain concluded by saying, 'Soil does not lie. It is your saviour. It is the motherland itself. A field that becomes fallow, is a portion of France that is dying. A fallow land once again cultivated, is a portion of France that is born again.'[18]

In addition to existing periodicals like *Urbanisme* that continued to be published during the war, new magazines dedicated to architecture, urban planning and engineering were created despite paper shortages. One of the very first issues of *Technique et Architecture* published in 1941 was entirely dedicated to sports, for instance, and it focused specifically on the green belt of Paris – the 'intellectual centre of France' that should spearhead Vichy's sports policy and build the country's most ambitious athletic infrastructure. Because space was so scarce in Paris proper, the Zone was logically earmarked to host the new sports facilities and playgrounds the city needed. This green belt would offer

> relaxation of the nerves, training of the muscles, resting for the eyes, developing of the chest, appeasing of the minds, all will come together and all will contribute to the physical and moral balance of a regenerated child population.[19]

In line with Pétain, many prominent space designers called for a renewed relationship to discipline and health, by way of physical education taking place in newly built open-air sports grounds and parks. 'Promoters of order, you will promote health at a time when our government is busy improving the race and commands you to build stadia and playgrounds,'[20] wrote the foremost landscape designer André Véra.

In 1943, the monthly periodical *Urbanisme* published their eighty-sixth issue on 'gardens and green spaces'. The editorial – written by Véra – called for a garden that would be the representation of 'beauty and order', one that should be an opportunity to create a 'discipline that would not be foreign, neither English nor Chinese, but properly French'.[21] Thus, 'the garden will surround us with strength and courage, and will give France back the honour it once had'.

In another issue of *Urbanisme*, Véra had written that nonnative plants should be banned to prevent the 'sad dark spots created by trees that are not from here, like the cedars of Lebanon'.[22] In Europe a plant is considered 'native' if it existed in a region's biotopes *before* 1492, and the beginning of the transatlantic trade. Plants that arrived after that time are considered 'neophytes', and in some cases, 'invasive' – terminology that established dodgy parallels between people and flora. Véra's crusade against foreign influence in landscape design has its origin across the Rhine, in Nazi Germany's 'mania for native plants'.[23] In Germany and in the countries they colonised, landscape design – which included the design of motorways and railways – became an intensely political, nationalist and racist endeavour that favoured a 'blood-and-soil-rooted garden', where 'native' plants are cherished while 'foreign' flora – and people – are hunted down like weeds.

Like Véra, the leading designer Henri Pasquier found direct inspiration in Germany's nationalist approach to road and landscape design, especially in the Reichsautobahnen programme, nicknamed *Straßen Adolf Hitlers* ('Hitler's roads'), that projected a novel network of motorways across Germany, one of the first major infrastructure endeavours launched by the Führer in 1933.

Motorways became an important artefact of the culture of Nazi Germany, represented in magazines, exhibitions and even paintings.

Not only were the new *Autobahnen* a technical modernist endeavour, but they also embodied a cultural and political engagement with space, with nature and therefore with the foundations of Germanic identity. The road was not antithetic to nature; it became part of nature, of a *völkischen Landschaft* – best translated as 'nationalist landscape' or 'ethnic landscape' – where the technical, aesthetic, political and cultural aspects of infrastructure and landscape merged to fulfil a political project, be it Hitler's or Pétain's.

In a previously mentioned 1943 issue of *Urbanisme*, several pages are dedicated to the Paris green belt. That year, the Paris administration launched a PR campaign where it proudly announced it had finally cleared the Zone of all its inhabitants, twenty-five years ahead of schedule. A few months after Pétain seized power, a new legal apparatus was enacted to remove all *zoniers*. It sped up the clearing of the Zone, facilitated compensations and funded urban planning works in Paris and specifically in the Zone.

The foreword to the law of 4 June 1941 specifically targeted the Zone, describing it as a 'leprous belt that brings shame to Paris' that needed to be redesigned as a 'belt of playgrounds, sports grounds and public promenades'. The country's architectural and planning elites rushed to annihilate the Zone and its *zoniers*, which had been described for decades as vermin, insects, immigrants, Jews and dangerous rebels threatening France and its values. They were weeds – *mauvaises herbes* – swarming in native plants, polluting the soil of France. And like weeds, they needed to be eradicated.

The fate of the Zone was a result of the questionable relationship between spatial design, social hygiene and racism that prevailed in France in the interwar period. The Zone was a 'slum', and its annihilation was the country planners' top priority – despite the war, despite the shortages, despite the urgent reconstruction programmes needed elsewhere. The conditions of this clearing remain to be studied. We do not know where the *zoniers* were relocated, we do not know how many they were, we do not know their names and their fates. The clearing of the Zone took place in an era of great violence, where French police took an active part in sending groups of people to certain death, including Jews, gays, Roma, Communists, resistants and all political opponents. Many questions remain for historians to answer.

Following Pétain's actions and just over two decades after the law of 1919, the Zone was almost entirely cleared out, ready to be rebuilt as green infrastructure, adorned with native species, playgrounds and stadia, to support the future of the French 'race' while maintaining the 'green buffer' between Paris and banlieue.

The year 1943 was also when an important report was published in which the city's engineers detailed for the first time their design for what they named a *boulevard périphérique*, a ring road. Authored by the head of Paris urbanism, René Mestais, the 195-page publication contains many illustrations, maps and graphs.[24] At a time of paper shortage, in the middle of a war in which resources were extremely scarce, the publication of such a report certainly demonstrates the urgency of the issue of traffic in the eyes of its author and the administration he headed.

The removal of the Zone had initiated the 'Renaissance of Paris', writes Mestais. For him there was both a practical and symbolic aspect to the ring road. Of course, it was about connecting the facilities on the green belt, as well as Paris and the adjacent suburban towns. But it was also about marking the difference in space between *la Capitale* (definite article, uppercase *C* in the report) and *une banlieue* (indefinite article, lowercase *b*, singular). The ring road was imagined as an element of the city pertaining to 'order and beauty' – the same expression used by André Véra in his 1941 manifesto. For Mestais, the Boulevard Périphérique was as much about improving road traffic as it was an urban planning endeavour that might be a catalyst to reinforce the buffer of the green belt between Paris proper and the banlieue. The idea of a green belt acting as a buffer between the prime real estate of Paris and the less attractive one of the banlieue remained active more than thirty years after the Dausset-Hénard debate.

After explaining that Paris never recovered from the 1860 annexation of suburban towns – that is, that these towns never quite became 'Parisian', and that insalubrious housing had remained in La Villette, Ménilmontant, la Chapelle – Mestais continues:

> It is important to avoid, at all costs, that Paris 'drowns' in a banlieue that would bog it down yet again for a century . . . This will be the role vested in the boulevard périphérique, to crown of its beautiful alignments of poplars, elms and planes, the Parisian territory. This magnificent 'ring' of greenery could be, by the way, bounded by high square towers, of symmetrical architecture, where the pairs would mark the great exits of the Capital. They would be equipped with powerful floodlights whose jewels of light would trace in the night, the magistral orb of 'Paris's crown'.

It is important to point out that these words are taken from the very first page of the section dedicated to the ring road, while considerations on its role for automobile traffic came only after. The ring road as part of the green belt was therefore, for him, foremost an urban design project and then a thoroughfare meant to improve traffic.

The vocabulary of the report evokes beauty ('elegant', 'magistral', 'magnificent'), power ('crown', 'orb') and even heroism or religion ('sacrifices'). To refer to Paris as the 'great European salon' was politically loaded at a time when a series of exhibitions held in 1941, 1942 and 1943, called *La France Européenne* ('European France'), was organised at the Grand Palais by the Vichy regime and when the collaborationist propaganda pushed the idea of a French nation at the heart of German-led Europe. The 'powerful floodlights' refer to Albert Speer's Cathedral of Light (*Lichtdom*), a key element of Nazi rally aesthetics also used in the Berlin Olympics of 1936. Meanwhile, the 'high square towers of symmetrical architecture' hint at key architectural styles associated with fascism, such as Stripped Classicism, but also brought up the early twentieth-century project of Maison-Tours ('House-Towers') imagined for Paris by Auguste Perret. They also conjure a medieval imaginary, that of fortifications protecting the city from barbaric invasions.

The vision of René Mestais in 1943 constituted the first proposal for a ring road around Paris. Yet the infrastructure of the ring road was not necessarily imagined as a physical obstacle but as a spatial mark – a boundary – between Paris proper and the rest of the metropolis. There was no ambition there to recreate the fortifications freshly razed to the ground. The 'ring' of leisure, sports and communication infrastructure that would come up on the Zone, finally cleared out by the Vichy police, would also be a catalyst for urban renewal in the suburbs.

A year later, in 1944, France was liberated – or 'liberated herself' according to the official narrative. This Gaullist interpretation also explains that for the four years of war, there were two Frances: the illegitimate collaborative France of Pétain in Vichy, and the lawful France of de Gaulle resisting from London. For several years there were two corpora of laws being developed in parallel, two heads of state, two armies and so forth. The official discourse, the story we still learned at school when I was a child, was the Liberation, soon followed by the establishment of the Fourth Republic in 1946, had constituted a clear break with Vichy. All that happened between July 1940 and August 1944 was cancelled. Gone. Forgotten. Buried.

It took a foreign scholar to challenge this version of history. Robert Paxton, an American historian who published *Vichy France: Old Guard and New Order* in 1972, opened a major historiographical breach. Vichy was not an 'anomaly'; it was an autocratic regime, technocratic to a certain extent, that had a tremendous influence on postwar France and specifically in architecture and planning. Vichy, for instance, created the Order of Architects with the law of 31 December 1940 and regulated the profession for the first time. Meanwhile, the law of 15 June 1943 constituted a sea change for urban planning and architecture. Among other elements, it created mandatory building permits (and restricted to the newly regulated profession of architects the exclusive rights to submit one to planning authorities).

Furthermore, while the decree of 27 October 1945 formally abolished the law of 1943, it simultaneously reinstated most of the content of that law and would remain in place until 1977, with the introduction of major new legislation on architecture. The legal framework devised by the Vichy regime continued after the war without much change and often with the same civil servants in place. Some of the regime's iconic urban design projects continued their journeys too, unscathed. The green belt around Paris was one example of this continuity.

But the green belt never quite happened. Only a portion of the stadia and playgrounds were delivered. They remain in use today. As a teenager, from my central Paris school in a densely populated neighbourhood with no sports grounds close by, I took the *métro* to the stadium at Porte de Bagnolet for my physical education classes. My classmates and I came back with our skin greasy and our lungs dark, for we had spent two hours exercising by the ring road. Here and there, all around Paris, sports grounds and playgrounds have been constructed from the 1930s until the 1950s. Yet most of the ambitious 'green' projects planned for the Zone were eclipsed by infrastructure of a new kind, one that quietly devoured all that came in its path.

'Alert, Paris is dying!' announced a brochure published by the president of the Council of Paris Bernard Lafay in 1954. In this publication, *Solutions to the Problems Faced by Paris: Traffic* – also known as Plan Lafay – the right-wing ex-GP, who became one of the most influential figures of postwar urban planning at Paris City Hall, first saluted the 'remarkable' work achieved by René Mestais and his team in 1943. Among the solutions he proposed was not, of course, the removal of cars from the city, as we would do today, but instead the creation of new high-speed thoroughfares going through and around Paris, including a brand-new ring road. The momentum Lafay created won over the council, which voted in favour of the construction of a ring road on the Zone in December 1954. To a certain extent, the project approved by the Council of Paris that day was still the design proposed by Mestais ten years before.

By now, reader, you should not be surprised that in 1954 a ring road was considered an integral part of a green belt. The road *was* landscape. It would be lined up with elms and poplars, elegantly outlining the edges of the city. Yet the project quickly experienced some profound changes, as it switched from a parkway to an urban motorway, the first of its kind in France. Indeed, by the time the first sections opened they had already become dated, and a new generation of engineers wanted to upgrade the hardware. No more pavement along the ring road, no more access from minor side roads. By becoming a motorway, the thoroughfare would exist independently from the surrounding urban fabric to which it was connected only via interchanges. But the trees did not disappear, only their *functions* changed. As a new technological vision of the city emerged in the 1950s – the city as an assemblage of technical networks, the city as infrastructure – a new understanding of trees and vegetation blossomed. Trees, like the city, became infrastructure.

We must get past the idea that postwar urban planning was a concrete-dominated vision. Politicians, inhabitants and city makers paid much attention to trees – their locations, their numbers. The scriptwriter René Goscinny and comic book artist Albert Uderzo captured that zeitgeist in the character of Idéfix, invented in 1963, a little dog who accompanies the beloved French hero Astérix and cries every time a tree is uprooted. The uprooting of trees was always a cause of scandal, leading to vehement protests and bad press. Reading the debates at the Municipal Council of Paris on the proposed ring road, one discovers that more pages are dedicated to the fate of trees than the actual design of the road itself. The number of trees cut down or saved by one given route versus another became a technical argument in its own right. Trees were precisely mapped and accounted for, including their species and the dates when they were planted.

And on the perspective drawings for the ring road, trees were omnipresent. Engineers even scribbled on the renders with green pencils to insist on the dense vegetation the project would create. Trees had a function. They were meant to block the noise from the traffic. Trees would grow, promised the engineers to people living in social housing a few metres from the busy road – just wait, and the saplings of today will be your protective wall of tomorrow. Did these engineers even believe in it? The green walls never materialised. And yet today the vegetation is omnipresent – if you care to look. Vegetation is everywhere, yes, but sickly, yellow, covered with the black soot from car exhaust. Trees planted fifty years ago have been left there to fend for themselves.

Trees under the ring road, by Porte de la Villette, in 2021.

The green spaces they were meant to constitute are usually covered with trash – debris from car crashes, empty bottles of water that drivers have thrown out their windows, and all the garbage brought over by the people who pass by. It accumulates there because it is an edgy place within an edgy space. It is the least desirable piece of real estate for the whole of Paris. And this is where all the green that features on the renders for the ring road survives.

Climate change, as it has evolved from a niche issue into a mainstream one after decades of mobilisation by activists and the scientific community, has turned all urban projects 'green'. Proposals are inevitably 'sustainable', 'carbon-free' and so on. The edges of Paris have not escaped that logic. For example, the '1,000 Trees' office and commercial centre, imagined as a 'bridge-building' over the ring road, won an architecture competition organised by the City of Paris to develop twenty sites across the city, and promised to plant 1,000 trees as part of their architectural project. Praised at the time, when nobody seemed to challenge the impossibility of planting 1,000 trees on concrete with virtually no soil, the project's building permit was eventually revoked at the end of 2022. Green is added value in a society where we all superficially care about nature and climate change.

In May 2022, Mayor of Paris Anne Hidalgo announced that she would turn the Boulevard Périphérique into a 'new green belt'. Her announcement came with old-fashioned hand-drawn renders that carried a 1980s vibe. They showed the ring road covered with trees, and progressively turned from an urban motorway into an actual boulevard – by reducing the number of lanes and adding pedestrian crossings and traffic lights.

Since her election in 2014, following her role as first deputy mayor in charge of urban planning in the administration of the previous mayor, Bertrand Delanoë (2001–14), Hidalgo has led a rather courageous openly anti-car policy. Chair of the global network of mayors called C40 – an initiative launched by then mayor of London Ken Livingstone in 2005 and then rebooted by the billionaire then mayor of New York Michael Bloomberg, who remains one of its major funders – from 2016 until 2020, she has had a demonstrative 'green' position. Her governing coalition includes the Greens too, even though they regularly express their doubts regarding the genuineness of her engagement: for instance, when she supports with all her determination the construction of new skyscrapers by the edges of the capital city, despite their ecological costs. Yet to reintroduce the idea of a green belt is a strange move when considering how this type of project has been the vehicle for so many ideologies over the last century, including the worst ones.

Of course, I am not saying that this new green belt is fascist. But what we learn from studying the history of the edges of Paris is that a tree has no politics. To plant trees, to turn the city 'green', is not a project in itself. It is the ideology behind the act that matters. The one question to ask is: for what purpose? Planting trees because they look nice, because they are pleasant to see, because they cool the city down, does not make an ecological project, because it does not challenge the status quo. Instead, it slows down the self-destruction of the capitalist city – by mitigating against the climatic cataclysms it has brought onto itself.

Planting trees by the ring road, appeasing this urban motorway and assuaging the boundary space between Paris proper and its suburbs will certainly benefit the motorway's immediate neighbours – which is great. But in the absence of a long-term strategy for social housing across the Paris metropolis, it will also be a tremendous catalyst for gentrification by pacifying the edges of Paris. While the sincerity of politicians across the political spectrum, as well as planners, architects and developers, when it comes to ecology is best left for another book, one cannot avoid noticing that planting trees acts de facto as a new device to push the most underprivileged Parisians further away from the city centre. Indeed, a new green belt.

3

Pink Belt, Red Belt: Working-Class Banlieue and the Fear of the Revolution

The strangely named Park of the Hill of the Red Hat, on the eastern edges of Paris proper is one of my favourite gardens. Ignored by most Parisians, this five-hectare neoclassical green space designed in the late 1930s by the architect Léon Azéma and his son, Jean, sits at the top of a hill named after a long-gone *guingette*, a dancing hall and café typical of the Zone. As you walk in via the main entrance, a red-brick cascade of water playing with the slopes of the terrain is topped with a callipygian statue of white stone referred to as *Eve* or *Welcoming Paris*. If you ascend to the top of the park, you will enjoy one of the most impressive views of the northeast banlieue of Paris. A rare open vista in this part of town, and a haven of peace in a bustling city.

Down the hill runs the ring road, then comes Le Pré-Saint-Gervais, one of the tiniest towns of the Paris region. Until Paris absorbed a large share of its territory in the 1920s, Le Pré-Saint-Gervais had within its boundaries the long hilly fields on which the park was later built, when it was still the Zone. In the 1910s and 1920s, the large open expanse of the Hill of the Red Hat was a regular meeting point for pacifists and socialists, conveniently located close to the working-class districts of Paris and the red cities of the banlieue, such as Le Pré-Saint-Gervais – headed by a socialist or Communist mayor since 1904 without interruption.

One of those meetings, held on 25 May 1913, brought thousands of demonstrators to the hill, on a beautiful spring day, to hear the leading figures of socialism and pacifism speak. The initial demonstration that was meant to be held in central Paris had been banned by the prefect of police, who was afraid it would turn into a riot. The gathering had regrouped on the margins of the city. The charismatic socialist leader Jean Jaurès was the star of the day and overshadowed the dozens of other speakers. There is a famous photograph from that day, of Jaurès atop a makeshift rostrum – adorned with Phrygian caps, fasces and a bright red flag – with his long white beard and bowler hat, haranguing the crowd in a desperate effort to save peace while Europe had already inexorably taken the path of war.

Jean Jaurès delivering his speech in Le Pré-Saint-Gervais on
25 May 1913. Photograph by Maurice-Louis Branger.

The Hill of the Red Hat, now this quiet garden surrounded by red brick social housing, is one of the unsung key sites of socialism in Paris. And from the top of the hill, you stand on the roof of Paris, to contemplate what is left of the Red Belt and the dream of seeing the working-class districts and blue-collar banlieue unite against the bourgeois of Paris, ready to storm the capital city one more time.

In this chapter I will tell the story of two belts – one pink, made of social housing, and one red, made of Communist cities – that cordoned off the edges of the capital, surrounding a bourgeois Paris besieged by the proletariat. Indeed, the political climate at the beginning of the 1920s was explosive. The Russian Revolution of 1917 was a beacon of hope for socialists across the globe that hoped to repeat the masterstroke. Then a few weeks after the armistice, in Germany, a Spartacist uprising was crushed by military groups who also murdered Rosa Luxemburg and Karl Liebknecht in January 1919. Meanwhile, in Paris, French Bolsheviks gathered considerable momentum for the violent overthrow of France's bourgeois power.

On 5 May 1919, the president of the Municipal Council of Paris gave the first pickaxe blow that started the deconstruction of the fortifications of Thiers. The military infrastructure that took four years to build would take more than a decade to be fully removed, and then an extra one to clear the Zone. In the initial convention signed in 1912, 3 per cent of the freed land was reserved for social housing; in 1913 an amendment had already increased that figure to 8 per cent, then 25 per cent with the law of 1919, which enacted its dismantlement. Eventually, in a national effort to promote the construction of social housing across France, the share of public housing to be built where the fortifications stood eventually reached a third of the future housing stock.

In France, like in most European countries at the time, the housing crisis was so dire that governments of all sides had stepped in to offer improved living conditions to their citizens and developed social housing en masse. The ambition was grounded in social aims (better, happier lives for the many instead of the few) and hygiene targets (limiting the rate of diseases, improving life expectancy, decreasing infant mortality). They were political too: offering affordable, decent housing limited the risk of anger, and therefore revolt, while concentrating the workers in specific building blocks and neighbourhoods that were easier to police. The objectives often intersected – for instance, the large thoroughfare and inner courtyards that provided light and air and that cleared away the miasma, as per hygienist principles, also allowed easy police and even military interventions. While the old, narrow streets of ancient Paris provided many nooks to hide in and secondary exits that the police did not know of, here the blueprint of the new buildings would be easily accessible, and all possible exits were mapped out.

The idea that the government and municipalities should provide housing and disrupt the private market had slowly matured since the 1880s. The first public social housing provider was created in August 1913 by the city of La Rochelle. Paris followed suit a few months later, in January 1914, with the creation of the Office public d'habitations à bon marché de la Ville de Paris – the Office for Affordable Housing of the City of Paris, or OPHBMVP. As you can see, the love of French administrative culture for obscure acronyms goes back a long way. This was a sea change. If today – however battered by several decades of neoliberalism – the idea of public housing might seem self-evident to us, at the time, the thought that cities were entrusted to be involved in the building and management of social housing for their most underprivileged constituents was revolutionary. It would have a profound impact on urban planning, especially in Paris. Around the same time as social housing law reached maturity, the future of the fortifications was settled. These two major social and architectural events unfolding concomitantly should have been the perfect storm for a profound reshaping of Paris space. But instead, the storm came from the east, and it smelled like black powder and mustard gas.

The menace of international conflict had been the pretext to erect the last fortifications of Paris. The first global conflict in the world's history would delay its removal by an extra decade – and be the chance for one last reactivation of the Thiers Wall, to no avail. On 3 August 1914, France and the German Empire were at war, by the end of the month Paris was being bombed and in the first days of September the German Army was within reach of the capital. From their camps outside the city, the German soldiers could see the Eiffel Tower. But the offensive failed, the German Army withdrew and Paris remained safe for the rest of the war, with combat raging further north.

At the end of the conflict, France was broken. One million four hundred thousand Frenchmen had died, 4 million had been wounded and 1.1 million would remain permanently disabled. More than 10 per cent of France's working population had been killed. Nine hundred Frenchmen had died every day of the war. To the list of the dead and the injured, one needs to add the birth deficit, estimated at 1.4 million babies who were never born. Four hundred thousand homes, located mainly in the north of France and in rural counties, had been destroyed.

France experienced a major housing deficit. The situation predated the war but became even more acute in the course of the conflict.

World War I was meant to be a short war: the Germans imagined themselves in Paris by Christmas 1914, and the French in Berlin by the same time. The initial emergency measures to support the war effort were constantly renewed and became a permanent state. This is how the momentum towards building social housing had been abruptly interrupted as all funds were redirected from construction to the war effort.

A moratorium on rents had been voted on in August 1914 just days after the global conflict broke out. Families of conscripts and modest households did not have to pay rent anymore if they had lost income because of the war. The moratorium was lifted in April 1918, as the French State partially compensated the loss for modest landlords. The destructions of the war, the suspension of investments in new constructions, the burden for some landlords who did not maintain their properties during the war and the reduction of the profit margins for private developers all contributed to the postwar housing crisis. But the nature of the housing crisis had changed, while the prewar debate focused on quality with campaigns against 'slums' and substandard housing, the problem had now become the sheer number of housing units available and the urgent need to deliver more. The housing crisis also concerned a wider scope of the French population: not only the working classes and the destitute, but the middle classes too.

To address the lack of funds available and the delay in the construction the state got involved directly, with cash subsidies to help social housing providers build more units faster, while setting up national housing targets. This new attitude towards production and hard figures reflected Taylorist principles applied to housing. In 1928 the Loucheur law established a five-year plan to build 260,000 housing units across France. But this law came too late. Right after the war, the government had preferred to maintain the status quo, for instance by financially supporting landlords and owner-occupiers to rebuild their properties as they were, instead of using this opportunity for more ambitious housing and urban planning reform.[1]

Five years after the vote of 1919 regarding the demolition of the fortifications, and as the deconstruction enterprise was progressing, the city architect Louis Bonnier presented to the municipal council a hybrid document – part masterplan, part policy – that envisioned the future of the fortifications. The space left free by the fortifications would be divided into plots of land sold to a variety of investors to build housing and infrastructure. About 67 hectares out of 444 were meant to be sold off to private developers. The income this operation generated was designed to balance the books of the whole operation.

The Louis Bonnier plan of 1924 did not have any ambition towards social welfare. Yes, a great amount of social housing was meant to be developed, as we will see in a moment, but this operation did not aim at redrawing the socio-economic maps of Paris. Because the programme required economic viability, the masterplan followed the rules of capitalism and reserved the prime real estate for the construction of luxury condominiums – for instance, the area close to the Bois de Boulogne, home to Paris's wealthiest neighbourhoods, then and now. Meanwhile, two types of subsidised homes were proposed: *habitations à bon marché* (HBM), social housing with subsidised rent meant for working classes, and *immeubles à loyer modéré* (ILM), affordable housing designed for the middle classes. Each would get their own city blocks, following similar patterns all along the edges of Paris: close to the improved and redesigned gates of Paris, the flats for the private market; the cheapest plots, those further away from the great gates, were meant for the most modest social housing units. A few days after the vote that approved the planning document for the fortifications, the first plots were cleaned out and sold off. Paris's most mammoth housing building programme of the century was about to begin.

The tragedy of World War I spurred on many technological developments. The aeroplane, for example. Bird's-eye views, photography shot from aircrafts, became common after the war, arguably contributing to planners' remote – and god-like – understanding of the city as a tissue that one can cut through, or a machine that needs fixing. The photographs shot in the interwar period of the construction site on the Zone offer a dramatic illustration of the ambition of this operation. Horizontal layers of cities created a Parisian patisserie with so many textures and tastes that one risked indigestion.

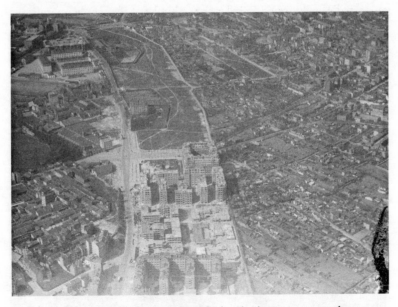

From the left-hand side to the right-hand side: Paris proper; the former fortifications being cleared and replaced by social housing; the Zone and the banlieue (Bagnolet). Photograph from 1931.

Starting from Paris and the clearly structured city proper, we see in the photographs the site of the former fortifications where tall buildings of eight or nine storeys were replacing the forts that, in some instances, still stand in the background as they await their final dismantlement. Between Paris proper and the new buildings, a widened Boulevard of the Marshals. Then comes the Zone, a dense fabric of makeshift houses and allotments, dotted with the odd industrial buildings. And finally, suburban municipalities, in all their diversity, were often made of a fabric of modest self-built houses, but also sometimes well-structured industrial ensembles.

A third of the lots of the former fortifications were attributed to social housing, built by the city's social housing provider: the Office for Affordable Housing of the City of Paris. The differences between

Social housing being built at Porte de Clignancourt and Porte de Saint-Ouen in 1929, with the Zone in the foreground.

the two types of flats – those for the working classes, and the others for the middle classes, mainly translated into the size of the rooms, the overall dimension of the flats and their equipment (for example, a bathtub in a larger bathroom or underground parking). A third category, for-profit flats by private developers, proposed luxury buildings aimed at an elite clientele.

Social housing being built at Porte d'Orléans in 1929.

The city's social housing companies offered a relatively novel way to build the city. First, instead of organising open architectural competitions, they relied on their own architecture departments. If the head architects in charge of supervising the design of entire city blocks made sure they entrusted each building to a different designer, the architectural language they used did not leave much room for autonomy and innovation. The social housing blocks that formed all around the city logically followed the principles of social hygiene: with a focus on air and sun. Yet their orientation was in relation to the Boulevard of the Marshals, instead of the amount of sunshine the flats would receive.

In lieu of the traditional Haussmannian blocks with their closed inner yards, the HBM offered open, connecting courtyards. The patterns, orientations and compositions of each block changed from one to another – yet the relative monotony and austerity of their design echoed strangely the military and police barracks that formerly dotted the space of the fortifications. As the programme continued throughout the 1920s and was amplified with the Loucheur law of 1928, its architectural ambitions shrank. There was less room for the rare design frivolities – brick motifs, innovative decorations – and the equipment that was imagined for each block was eventually left out. The libraries, free clinics, washhouses, kindergartens and schools were progressively removed from the construction programme – though most blocks maintained their playgrounds for children. With time, the project was rationalised further. Economics was key here – profits needed to be maxed out to balance the account and land was limited. Buildings were built higher, creating darker apartments on the first floors, and their footprints were increased to fill as much of the dedicated plots as possible, leaving less room for green spaces and shared amenities.

Brick was the housing complexes' dominating material, to the extent that the 38,000 housing units built on the former fortifications were nicknamed the 'brick belt' of Paris, or more poetically its 'pink belt'. Brick was not a familiar sight in Paris at the time, where Haussmannian buildings had traditionally been built with cream-coloured cut stones made of Lutetian limestone. Despite the quality of the material used for constructing the HBM, brick was not considered a noble building material. The brick-clad HBM were associated at the outset with subpar construction; they stood out as housing for the poor, while the bourgeois lived in cut-stone buildings.

With their concrete-made structural elements, which made possible a fast pace of construction, the HBM used modern techniques but delivered them in an artisanal way. The 1920s were a period of intense innovation in architecture and construction that the HBM did not embrace. For instance, Le Corbusier's Dom-Ino concept house of 1914–15 imagined prefabricated concrete elements that could form the structural framework of a modular, quick-to-build dwelling. None of the key innovative French or Paris-based architects of the time – Robert Mallet-Stevens, Hector Guimard, Donat Alfred Lagache, André Lurçat, Henri Sauvage – were invited to design for the public housing office. Spearheaded by Le Corbusier, the International Congress of Modern Architecture (CIAM) attempted to construct a building on the bastion Kellerman, south of Paris, for the 1937 International Exhibition of Art and Technology in Modern Life, but these efforts also failed.

The HBM programme was quickly critiqued by the architectural elites as a missed opportunity, both in its artistic ambitions and the technology used. For decades, designers had imagined a variety of architectural futures for the space where the former fortifications had been. And now, they had to witness a boring, slightly dated, unambitious programme rise into the sky. The feeling of frustration was probably a genuine disappointment for the future of Paris and architecture at large, mixed with personal bitterness to have been left out of this grand enterprise. Some buildings were almost copy-pasted from one block to another, accentuating the monotony of the brick belt: for instance the 7 Rue Changarnier in the twelfth arrondissement, and the 9 Rue Abel Ferry in the sixteenth.

The reception was, at best, cold. The programme of HBM, delivering close to 40,000 housing units over a decade, was often simply ignored by the profession. Otherwise, it was riled: 'It is a desert for the heart and the spirit,' writes Le Corbusier in 1938, 'it is an immense, gigantic failure, an abyss of disappointment.'[2] Commentators mocked the lack of insulation from noise as well as the overall design. The Franco-Swiss writer Blaise Cendrars wrote that 'those walls are made of papier-mâché (and I mean it literally, like some loo roll that would have been chewed after use)'.[3] He concludes: 'We still have the sound of the garbage bins being taken out that is very much [French], otherwise it feels like we're in Czechoslovakia considering how everything has been rationalised in a very basic way.'

Yet one must be careful about historians' account of the programme's reception. Yes, the houses were disappointing, boring and repetitive, and they suffered from a lack of ambition. But the scheme also ensured that houses were built quickly, providing tens of thousands of Parisians modern homes with gas, electricity, hot and cold water, a kitchen, a bathroom and inner courtyards for play. Overall, very decent homes. If the cultural elite of the country was disconcerted and frustrated, the thousands of Parisians that moved in, with more modest expectations, were by and large content. There is no trace in the archives of great movements of protest, of riots or of disappointments.

Some of the first buildings built there have just turned one hundred years old. Some of their inhabitants have reached this milestone too, and they have not left, nor have any desire to. I remember visiting a friend of my parents there when I was a child. Dorothée was a retired German teacher, in her eighties at the time. She had lived in an HBM since the 1950s, when she moved in with her husband. It was a cosy flat with parquet; the rooms were not big, but they were warm, with a view over the ring road in the distance. All in all, a charming flat. The HBM were boring and remain so, but they offered decent housing conditions to the many, and a home to love – to such an extent that for some of their residents, it has been their life's home.

Yet in terms of urban planning, there was not much to save the HBM programme. It had done nothing to connect banlieue and Paris. Quite the opposite, it had become exactly what many feared: another wall between Paris and the suburbs, a stark underlining of the city's edges. The cordon of social housing blocks structured around cleanly designed open courtyards reflected the ambivalence of social reform and urban planning: by offering better, nicer, brighter flats to the workers, it had certainly improved their everyday lives and comfort; yet by removing the 'slums' of central Paris it constituted a new push – fifty years after Haussmann – to kick out the working classes from the city's older districts. In doing so, unwillingly, it reinforced the myth of a wealthy, reactionary, bourgeois Paris surrounded by a proletariat that was building up the strength and the rage to take down the gates of Paris and flood into the capital city. For, in the eyes of the Communists in the banlieue, their class enemies still held the rifles.

'The Workers of the Paris Region Have Voted for the Revolution', and in all caps, 'IN THE BANLIEUE WE BEAT ALL THE BOURGEOIS ALLIANCES', read the front page of the 24 May 1924 edition of the Communist newspaper *L'Humanité*. 'Hail to the 300,000 Parisian soldiers of the Revolution!' wrote Marcel Cachin, the director of the newspaper and member of the French Communist Party's political bureau, in his editorial. The legislative elections of May 1924 were a major surprise victory for the young Communist Party. While the national results were rather disappointing, with less than 10 per cent of the votes, the outcomes in Paris went beyond what political observers had anticipated, with 26 per cent of the votes in the capital city's immediate suburbs. Yet more than Cachin's, it was another piece published on that same page by the journalist and Member of Parliament Paul Vaillant-Couturier that would leave an imprint on Paris's political and spatial imaginary for the rest of the century.

> Around Paris, a large red spot is sprawling. The revolutionary victory, from a strategic point of view, is undeniable. Paris, the capital city of capitalism, is surrounded by the proletariat that is growing aware of its own might. *The faubourgs of Paris are back!*

Four years of World War I had transformed Vaillant-Couturier into a firebrand and excellent orator. He had joined the army as a dandy and passionate Catholic but came home an ardent socialist and pacifist. Conjuring up the historical figure of the riotous working-class *faubourgs*, the towns right outside the eighteenth-century fortifications of Paris, the article by Vaillant-Couturier titled 'Paris, Surrounded by the Revolutionary Proletariat' came up with that key image that defined the relationship between bourgeois Paris and its working-class suburbs for the rest of the twentieth century: a series of red bastions were gearing up to storm the old bourgeois city and carry out the revolution. Red like the flag of the Paris Commune, red like the blood of revolutionaries, red like communism. He concludes:

> The success of [this election], holds within it the strength of the revolutionary proletariat to control the reactionary districts of the centre, its banks, its state monuments, its food supplies, its roads, its military barracks . . . And now, to work comrades! . . . You have put your votes in the ballot box, but your class enemies still hold the rifles.

These were not empty words. Written a mere eight years after the Russian Revolution of 1917, Vaillant-Couturier's article reflected a belief in the eventuality of a proletarian uprising in Paris, and then France, which was a realistic aspiration for a Communist party in its infancy that had broken off from mainstream socialism four years prior.

On 25 December 1920, the French Section of the Workers' International (SFIO) met in Tours, a mid-sized town three hours from Paris. The city was meant to be a 'neutral' ground for socialists to congregate as they decided the future of their political strategy. Recent violent strikes questioned the role of unions and their political positions, while the socialists were split between those who supported the Second International, who had backed up the war – betraying pacifism, at the heart of socialism's ethos; and the others who sought to cut ties with the former and join the Comintern or Third International, which had been founded in March 1919 in Moscow under Lenin's leadership. To leave the Second International and join the Third meant a radical reevaluation of socialist strategies at home and a commitment to the absolute dictatorship of the proletariat, together with an allegiance to Moscow. At Tours, the final chasm was achieved. With two-thirds of the votes, the majority broke off from Léon Blum's SFIO to create what would become the French Communist Party, which adhered to the Third International. While the SFIO lost many of its members, it retained within its ranks the majority of socialist elected officials. *L'Humanité* newspaper chose its sides too: communism over socialism.

The elections four years later were the first legislative or municipal elections since the Tours Congress. Nationally, the Cartel des Gauches, an alliance of left-leaning parties, won the elections. The SFIO that took part in the alliance sent 106 MPs to the Palais Bourbon, the home of the National Assembly. It was the first time socialists won as part of an alliance, even though they did not take an active part in governing. The Communist Party obtained close to 900,000 votes out of 9 million voting men (women were granted the right to vote only in 1944) and had twenty-six MPs, of which nine were in Paris and the banlieue.

A year after the legislative elections of 1924, local elections took place across France. Once again, it was not the 'red wave' that the Communists had hoped for, but the Communist Party did manage to win elections in six cities of the Paris region, on top of the three they already controlled – because mayors had switched from SFIO to PCF after the Tours Congress. While Saint-Denis, adjacent to Paris, was taken away from SFIO candidates, five other cities were conquered over right-wing candidates: Clichy, Malakoff, Vitry-sur-Seine, Villejuif and Ivry-sur-Seine.

Ivry-sur-Seine, which, as I write these lines, has been Communist for close to a century, would become the flagship Communist town of France. Georges Marrane, a clockmaker and mechanic who had joined the political bureau of the party in 1922 and played an active role in the Communist leadership, was parachuted into Ivry and elected mayor in 1925. As the historian Emmanuel Bellanger explains, the first years of administration were both conflicted and conflictual.[4] The issues were not only in the Communist aediles' relationship to the bourgeois state and their representatives but also in their relation to the party that acted as the guardian of the Communist ethos and Bolshevik discipline while being suspicious of any individual emerging from its ranks. A peculiar mode of government, between the devil of 'collaboration' and the deep red sea of Bolshevik ideology, emerged in the Red Belt of Paris: municipal communism.

The initial strategy of 'class against class', of open and direct opposition, offered no room for negotiation or compromise. Any deviance would be severely reprimanded by the party. But the reality was more complex: Communist mayors had to adapt to the realpolitik of managing major urban towns on the edges of the great capitalist city. For instance, even though it was his privilege as a newly elected mayor, Georges Marrane did not dismiss local civil servants when he sat down behind the mayor's office at Ivry city hall, but instead compromised and worked with those who knew the city best. Quickly, mayors – and the party – had to accept public subsidies from the bourgeois state and, therefore, mingle with their representatives.

Bellanger recounts a telling episode when in July 1925, a few months after their elections, the city's town hall had to be renovated. Eighty per cent of the cost was meant to be borne by the *département*. The Communist position should have been to renounce the money, in order to avoid the 'class collaboration' that it entailed. And some among the councillors at Ivry did oppose the collaboration. But why renounce all this money and bring this financial burden onto Ivry residents? Communist principles were set aside, and the delegation that included civil servants of the prefecture, conservative councillors and the head of the *département*, André Morizet – excluded from the Communist Party in 1923 – was received courteously by the mayor and his administration, and the funding granted.

Communist mayors had to respect the law while serving a party whose official line was to take down the bourgeois republic. Symbolic, short-lived yet powerful gestures and their reprimand by the establishment became opportunities to demonstrate mayors' opposition to the bourgeois state and their faithful adhesion to communism. This was the case when the mayor of Ivry flew the red flag, instead of France's, on the town hall facade. It is said Marrane eventually bowed and removed the red flag, but replaced it with only a tiny tricolour one.

Mayors had to administrate their local governments efficiently and lawfully, and this necessarily meant bending the Marxist-Leninist dogma – for instance, by not cancelling the octroi tax on food, even though the Communist line made it a priority to remove the tax. Marrane also renounced municipalising certain services – such as the undertakers, or the gas and electricity providers. The practice of local power meant 'municipal communism' would not be about creating revolutionary outposts all around Paris, but offering exemplary infrastructure, excellent architecture and a superior quality of life to the workers.

If the mayors of the Red Belt followed a complex path between the ideology and the realpolitik of everyday administration, the image of the threat constituted by Communist cities was perpetuated by the press and politicians of both sides: the Communists were eager to demonstrate they remained a revolutionary party seeking to topple the bourgeois state, while their opponents were anxious to remind their voters of the dangerous threat on the country's institutions and stability that the Bolsheviks represented. In the Communist sphere, Ivry earned its reputation as an 'offensive and subversive red bastion' in August 1928, when the city was meant to hold an 'antimilitarist' and 'anti-imperialist' demonstration that had been forbidden by the prefect of police.[5]

While *L'Humanité* called for the demonstration to take place, despite its unlawfulness, and offered a map of the different key places to meet on the front page of its edition of 5 August 1928, conservative press, such as the newspaper *Le Figaro*, denounced 'the Bolshevik threat' that used the demonstration as 'an excuse to have the workers

25e ANNÉE — N° 10825   SERVICE GRATUIT   DIMANCHE 5 AOÛT 1928

RÉSERVISTES DE LA 22° !
Demain 6 août
départ de la 1re série
pour les 21 jours
d'entraînement
à la guerre...

l'Humanité

ORGANE CENTRAL DU PARTI COMMUNISTE (S.F.I.C.)
FONDATEUR : JEAN JAURÈS   LE NUMÉRO : 30 CENTIMES

...DANS LES CAMPS
DANS LES CENTRES-MOBILISÉS
MANIFESTEZ contre
les périodes
LUTTEZ avec vigueur
contre la préparation
de la guerre impérialiste

A IVRY QUAND MÊME !

AUX TRAVAILLEURS FRANÇAIS ET ETRANGERS AUX SOLDATS ET MARINS

LE PROLÉTARIAT PARISIEN CONTRE LE COUP DE FORCE

Hier soir, au Cirque de Paris dix mille prolétaires ont crié : « A Ivry ! »

LA FOULE IMMENSE, DRESSÉE CONTRE LA TRAHISON DES CHEFS SOCIALISTES, S'ENGAGE A COMBATTRE PAR TOUS LES MOYENS LA GUERRE IMPÉRIALISTE MENAÇANTE

Vaillant-Couturier arrêté

La foule hier soir au Cirque de Paris

DERNIÈRE PROVOCATION

150 arrestations

La manifestation d'Ivry

BARTHOU L'HOMME DES 3 ANS VEUT SA JOURNÉE

Il deviendrait Capdeville de ses fonctions de police municipale

MALGRÉ LE CARNAGE POLICIER ET NOTRE PROPAGANDE LE PROLÉTARIAT SE DRESSERA CONTRE LA GUERRE

L'interdiction de Barthou

La maire d'Ivry dessaisi

La chasse aux étrangers

PAR-DESSUS L'ATLANTIQUE

Sans nouvelles certaines des deux aviateurs polonais

DEUX NAVIRES LES AURAIENT APERÇUS

Mais on suppose, d'après leur position, qu'ils ont renoncé à gagner New-York.

DEUX CONGRÈS INTERNATIONAUX

Bruxelles et Moscou

par Marcel CACHIN

A 14 h. 30, trois grands meetings

Front page of L'Humanité, dated 5 August 1928, displaying the map for the 'Battle of Ivry' (bottom left-hand corner).

of the Parisian region rebel against the army and the country, and to continue, as per the instructions received from Moscow, their preparation for a civil war'.[6] The police preemptively stormed the city, locked up all municipal facilities to forbid any gatherings and arrested all men getting off the tramway carriages, as well as those that loitered in the streets. The operations, supervised by the prefect of police himself, Jean Chiappe, led to 1,339 arrests – according to the police – and up to 2,000 according to *L'Humanité*.

The day before, a gathering at the Cirque d'Hiver in central Paris, had stirred up the crowd. Communist leaders had taken the stage one after the other to denounce imperialism, colonialism and France's intention to declare a future war against the USSR. Once again, the speech by Paul Vaillant-Couturier stood out, as he explained:

> Global capitalism is gearing up for a war against this country that stands as its nightmare because it is for all peoples a source of hope: the Soviet Republic. All capitalist nations are reconciled in the hatred against the Soviets and the red army . . . What they can't forgive us is that we are this red army! . . . The proletariat cannot have its right to protest taken away in a city that it has conquered . . . TOMORROW YOU WILL ALL BE IN IVRY TO DEMONSTRATE AGAINST WAR![7]

Arrested as he left the meeting on Saturday night, Vaillant-Couturier was released on Sunday evening once the demonstration in Ivry had failed. The Battle of Ivry had been cut short by the prefect of police of Paris, preemptively striking with all his might.

The history of communism in the banlieue is connected to another riotous event that took place a few years later, on 6 February 1934. But it was not one led by the far left, but instead by the far right.

Prefect of Police Jean Chiappe was fired at the beginning of February 1934 following a major political and financial scandal, the Stavisky affair (whose recount would lead us too far away from our concern in this chapter). Chiappe was as much loved by the conservatives and the far right as he was loathed by the left and the Communists, for he had the reputation of being quite lenient with the former and harsh with the latter. His firing came after weeks of reactionary protests and political instability. In response, a constellation of far-right organisations – including French fascists, monarchists, veterans, etc. – called for a demonstration on the Place de la Concorde, right across the Seine River from the National Assembly. The most powerful of these organisations was Action Française, an anti-republican monarchist movement created in 1899 during the Dreyfus affair whose ambition was to topple the French Republic.

The gathering turned into a march and then into riots, as protesters tried to storm the National Assembly. The fights continued throughout the night, and police forces opened fire several times. Among the protesters, 12 died by firearms, and 657 were injured. One soldier was killed, and 1,664 others were wounded. The crisis would lead the government to fall, replaced by right-wing leaders – including Marshal Pétain, appointed minister for the first time.

Left forces – militants and leaders alike – interpreted the violent event of February 1934 as a genuine fascist coup attempt that narrowly failed. This shakeup convinced the Communist leaders to give up their 'class against class' strategy to form an alliance with the 'collaborationists' of the SFIO as well as the Radical Party (traditionally left-wing). The upheaval this alliance constituted cannot be overstated. Over several weeks, the most fundamental element of the political strategy of the French Communist Party was overturned – with the necessary approval of Moscow. The danger of fascism in

France was too strong to continue fighting for left-wing values as fragmented parties. The profound shift was validated by the congress of the Communist Party held in Ivry in June 1934.

The year 1934 must have been very destabilising for all Communists, but the target had been clearly set: the left was united against fascism. And that included being against fascists at home, against Hitler in Germany, against Dolfuss in Austria, and against Mussolini in Italy. The same edition of *L'Humanité* that recounted secretary general Maurice Thorez's long report to the congress on the party's new political line, actually displayed on its front page in a much more cheerful and celebratory way, the alliance signed between the Communists and socialists of Paris, who called for a meeting on 2 July in the city centre.

Two 'red waves' followed the reconciliation. The municipal election of 1935 was a 'red' triumph in Paris while the legislative elections of 1936 saw the appointment of a socialist-led government, with Léon Blum as prime minister. This was the first socialist government in France, and the first time the Communists were part of the majority – even though they did not take part in the government, just as the socialists had done when they formed an alliance with the radicals in 1925. The years of the Popular Front remain to this day a foundational event for the history of France, when, following massive strikes across the country, major social rights were granted: paid holidays, the increase of wages by 12 per cent on average, the nationalisation of railway companies to form the SNCF, a legal limit of forty hours of work per week. The municipal elections brought victories for the Communists, the socialists and their allies.

From nine cities, the Communists now led twenty-seven, the socialists had nine, and the rest of their allies had an extra ten in the Paris region. The Communists were now in charge of 718,000 souls, and even though the insurrectionist messages had been toned down, *L'Humanité* ran this headline on its front page: 'Victory for Liberty! Hail the Red Belt of Paris!' Not only did the image of the Red Belt remain vivid, but Paris and the working-class suburbs had truly become a key asset for the party's strategy. Indeed, the party had a concentration of masses of voters there, and – in the event of a revolution – the hundreds of thousands of Communist sympathisers lived within walking distance of the key institutions of the country.

Last but not least, in 1936 Marrane, the Communist mayor of Ivry, was elected president of the General Council of the Seine by his peers – that is, the president for the assembly bringing together all municipalities of the Seine department, a very important metropolitan role.

Other red waves followed, always at times of alliance with other political parties of the left: in 1945, right after the war, and before the Communists were kicked out of the government in 1947 (including Marrane, who had become minister for 'public health and the population'), and again in 1977, four years before the election of François Mitterrand as the first socialist president of the Fifth Republic. In 1977, there were 126 mayors in the Paris region – the red spot described by Vaillant-Couturier in 1924 was at its acme, but it was about to slowly disintegrate.

The title of Marrane's ministerial appointment was in direct line with his achievement as mayor. The party campaigned on their accomplishments as 'good administrators' of French cities, in the Paris region and across France. The propaganda film *Conquering Happiness*, 'directed by a team of Communist technicians' as the opening credits announced, which was released ahead of the 1947 municipal elections, offers a good illustration of their positioning. It features a list of achievements by Communist aediles with a clear message: Communist mayors get it done.

From the municipalisation of utility companies to Communist administrations' resourcefulness even in times of shortages, and their efficiency at achieving change, the documentary lists the policies set up since the 1920s. From Paris to Gennevilliers, Villejuif to Martigues, Calais to Ivry, the documentary covers a wide range of 'hard' and 'soft' infrastructure – as we would call them today – that the Communists had put in place. Social housing, swimming pools and stadia, free clinics, *goûters* for the elderly, new schools.

Politically, the towns of the Red Belt did not become little Soviets. Nor did they seek to achieve a Communist utopia in their architecture and urban planning. There were a few exceptions – for instance, the Karl Marx School in Villejuif designed by modernist architect André Lurçat. The British novelist Aldous Huxley who was commissioned to write a series of reportages on France for the magazine *Paris-Soir* in 1935 used the Villejuif school as the representation of an 'ideal of "social service", the ideal of what should be corporative life' while he denounced the sprawl of detached houses in the banlieue: 'the most hideous and shameful result of pure individualism's ethics'. As the historian Jean-Louis Cohen explains, the school had been the subject of much propaganda by the Communists, but the ambition invested in it had remained an exception, and André Lurçat spent the following years working in Moscow instead of cities of the Red Belt.[8]

The working-class banlieue, like their inhabitants, were castigated, stigmatised. But the Communists turned this stigma into pride by constructing the myth of the *banlieue rouge*, the red suburb, offering a flagship identity to the Parisian proletariat, what the historian Annie Fourcaut described as 'localist patriotism based on class'.[9] The banlieue rouge became a lifestyle, an identity associated with working-class life. More than urban planning, this manifested in the social rhythm of everyday life: the workplace, the party, the reading and selling of *L'Humanité*, the purchase of castles in the French countryside by Communist towns to offer summer camps to its youth (that is to say, the reappropriation of the ultimate symbol of the aristocracy for the children of the proletariat), afternoon tea for the elderly, theatre clubs, sports clubs – all instilled with a tiny dose of the soviet republic.

Furthermore, the USSR was never far: it was in the gift stamped 'Made in USSR' that children received at school for good grades, in the books 'printed in Moscow', in the pictures that were prevalent in the lives of the inhabitants of the red banlieue. It was in the memories too – for instance, the visit of Yuri Gagarin in June 1963 to Ivry, where there was a social housing complex named after him. An immense crowd welcomed the great Soviet hero. I remember the visit too. I was not born, but I grew up with stories of my mother receiving a kiss on the cheek from the great astronaut.

After the war, the Red Belt got 'redder' while the global political stage slowly restructured around the logic of the Cold War. In 1958, de Gaulle returned to national leadership with a new constitution and 'full powers' (as will be discussed in the next chapter). Urban planning projects in Paris and the spatial reorganisations of the whole region became his administration's pet projects – he personally reviewed the thorniest issues and pushed for profound reforms against the will of most local elected officials. The anticommunism of de Gaulle and his partisans was fierce. The myth of the insurrectionist Red Belt created in the 1920s had now turned into a defiance for the enemy 'from within', for all the 'little Moscows' surrounding the capital city.

The new constitution's author and de Gaulle's inaugural prime minister, Michel Debré, denounced the risk of 'erecting local [Communist] fortresses that would, in the future, make the issues created by this immense banlieue always more difficult for the nation'.[10] In an interview he gave in 1975, high-level civil servant Paul Delouvrier, who had been transferred from his post as general governor of Algeria to be appointed by decree in 1961 as the first head of the newly created Paris district, denounced in the most heinous terms this 'disgusting banlieue where the Communists thrived on the misery and filth of the suburbs' and concluded: 'We needed to improve their living conditions.'[11] De Gaulle wanted to 'break' this banlieue rouge, 'for the honour of France', said Delouvrier.

The threat was imminent. At the beginning of the 1960s, the Communists were close to establishing durable control of the *département* of the Seine. Now, as the Communists and the socialists gained more power, there was a true chance that they could seize the presidency and retain it for years. France's most powerful, wealthiest and largest city, the place where all the country's key political institutions were located, was about to be taken over by the Communists.

In a radical move to prevent such an outcome, de Gaulle's government proceeded to disband the Seine *département* created by the French Revolution and broke down the Paris region into seven new *départements*. In an anachronistic move echoing the Thiers Wall construction, the Paris region was chopped down into several smaller entities at a moment of great growth that demanded to imagine new, bigger regional bodies. This 'Balkanisation' of the Paris region was clearly targeted against the Communists to limit their power. They would never be able to seize Paris now, but they were 'granted' one red citadel: the *département* of Seine-Saint-Denis, number 93.

The political map drawn by de Gaulle's government meant that conservatives would never be able to regain Seine-Saint-Denis, but in return the Communists would never take control of the whole Paris region. The *neuf-trois*, as the Seine-Saint-Denis inhabitants proudly call their *département*, was a new manifestation of the banlieue rouge. But instead of becoming a proud red citadel, it would eventually embody the progressive collapse of the Communist Party, together with the fading of a working-class identity, and all the issues faced by suburban territories after the economic crisis of 1973 and the deindustrialisation that followed.

I had set up a meeting: a rendezvous with my mother. We meet at Porte d'Ivry, and first catch up over a meal at La Bretelle, a hip but laidback restaurant that *she* read about, nested under an interchange of the ring road. A surprising spot for Paris, and another testament to the fact that the unloved edges of the city are slowly gentrifying, becoming trendy, atypical, sought-after locations. We drink our coffees while contemplating the lower deck of the ring road – and eventually head for Ivry, the reason why we have met today.

I have asked her to walk with me on the streets of the 'red capital city', where she grew up in the 1950s and 1960s, and share her memories of growing up in a banlieue rouge. We stroll along the Seine, between a mall and a cement factory. The riverbanks here are neither charming nor romantic. They are mostly industrial, occupied by the plants that feed concrete to the building sites of Greater Paris. Further down is Ivry Harbour where commercial buildings and office spaces have progressively replaced the brownfields and brick-made factories. We take Rue Lénine, and walk up to the city centre, passing by the Cité Maurice Thorez. It is a beautiful social housing complex made of bright red bricks built in 1953, one of the first high-rise buildings in Ivry, modern and luminous.

My mom – her first name is Annick, but everybody calls her by her last name, Prime – tells me tenants there were the first to get open-plan kitchens, which we call *cuisine américaine*. The ensemble is T-shaped, in honour of the namesake of MP for Ivry and leader of the Communist Party Thorez – or so says the local lore. Down the same avenue, we go through the brutalist star-shaped ensemble by Renée Gailhoustet and Jean Renaudie completed in 1975. Its architecture – distinctive, convoluted and fascinating – is in a poor state, the concrete has decayed, glass is broken, the interior commercial gallery is made up of vacant shop units.

We manage to exit the Stars of Ivry – the name of the building – after hitting dead ends several times, then take the Rue Marat. Together with Saint-Just and Robespierre, Jean-Paul Marat, assassinated in his bathtub by the reactionary firebrand Charlotte Corday in 1793, was associated with some of the most radical elements of the French Revolution of 1789. Discreetly left aside by the state-backed history that does not know how to handle their contradictory heritage and loathed by the conservatives, these figures have been reclaimed as the intransigent heroes of the revolution by the Communists and the far left. All have streets named after them in Ivry. And indeed, we reach our destination: the Cité Robespierre-Marat, a beautiful, recently renovated social housing complex made of cream-coloured bricks where my grandparents lived from 1947 until their deaths, respectively in 1985 and 1995, with my two uncles and mother.

I grew up in central Paris, away – geographically and historically – from the red suburbs. But I heard the stories of this red 'paradise': the benefits of socialism without Soviet dictatorship; Yuri Gagarin's visit, which I have already mentioned; my grandma, who died a Stalinist; the reading of *L'Humanité* at home; my mum and her mother selling *Le Travailleur*, the local Communist newspaper – 'In the *cité* most people bought it', she explains; my uncle from Poland who joined the International Brigades in Spain to fight fascism; the Lubitel camera made in the USSR my mother received as a school prize with instructions engraved in Cyrillic characters. It is the first time I am back in Ivry since we cleared my grandparents' flat, nearly thirty years ago. My mother does not come often either.

Nothing has changed much since her childhood, but everything is different. The *cité*'s courtyard was filled with kids: 'We played all day long here,' she explains. We enter the building where she lived, number 15 – no locks on the main entrance, the way it was originally designed. Actually, the door, the letterboxes, the intercom, nothing has changed.

Further up we reach the allotments: how many times have I heard stories about my granddad's vegetables that fed the family all year long? The allotments are still there, up the glacis and down the moat of the military fort of Ivry – still owned by the army, who has tolerated the gardens since the 1920s. It is my first time here, and my mother has not been back since the 1970s. It is a rather large plot, and at the far end the same garden shed. 'We spent every Sunday here – I hated it.' On this sunny summer day, the setting is beautiful and charming. The architecture of the housing and the toponymy are echoes of the red Ivry of yesteryear. 'I think access to culture is what made red suburbs different,' says my mum: 'We had a theatre, a (municipal) cinema – that played the Soviet movie *The Cranes Are Flying* for its opening night.' Communism was a diffuse presence, with limited propaganda and no indoctrination. Not a little Moscow, though they liked to play with this image.

Red suburbs continue to exist somehow. About thirty towns in Paris are headed by a Communist mayor today. But the decline has been constant and inexorable. The red working-class culture in Paris disintegrated together with the industrial fabric of France. My family, like many others, who had voted Communist by habit for half a century, progressively stopped to put a *coco*'s name in the ballot box. In Ivry, the shop unit the Communist Party owned in my mother's *cité* is still there – but the freshly applied posters for the Fête de l'Humanité have been carelessly glued on the windows, and the door is boarded up.

4

Dirt Belt: Technocracy at Work in Paris

The shutters have been kept half-closed and the curtains are drawn. The spacious living room is shady, with a brown faux-leather sofa by the wall, while the rest of the furniture is all wood, lacquered with a dark veneer. Nobody is paying attention to the flat-screen TV playing an old, boring German police show dubbed in French, and the uncreased complete works of Aragon are lined up in a glass-door cabinet. My host sends her son away – he had paid an unannounced and untimely visit – turns off the TV and offers me a coffee. A heat wave, the second this summer of 2022, is crushing Paris, but the flat of Lucie Lapuszanska is cool, cosy and quiet. I turn my recorder on.

When the inhabitants of the Cité Fougères, a social housing complex on the edges of Paris as it touches on Bagnolet, moved in at the beginning of the 1960s, they found a peaceful setting, brand-new flats and modern comfort. Lucie, a single mom who squatted a derelict building on Rue des Couronnes with her baby son, fought to get one of those apartments despite the administration's initial decision that she did not qualify for rehousing. 'If you're defeatist from the get-go, you'll get nothing!' she said. She won, and in 1963 moved in. Lucie is a fighter, she spent a lifetime fighting: for better housing conditions, for a new bus stop in the *cité*, against evictions, against injustice. Her high-pitched, raspy voice bears the scar of another fight: laryngeal cancer. She won this battle too, but the combat is always on. Slight, gnarled, strong, the energetic eighty-one-year-old fills the room.

'I started asking myself questions as a child', she explains. It was during a demonstration organised by the Communist Party to protest the visit of General Matthew Ridgway, nicknamed 'Ridgway the Plague' by the Communist press, who accused him of having used biological weapons against North Koreans and Chinese soldiers as commander of North Atlantic Treaty Organisation (NATO) forces in the Korean War. Ridgway was about to take over from Eisenhower and become Supreme Allied Commander of Europe for NATO, which had its headquarters in Paris at the time. Lucie saw the police charging; a woman – 'a granny' – fell on the ground, and the police clubbed her. 'Probably she wasn't a granny! But I was ten ... Needless to say, when I got back to school the day after, I made a big deal out of it!' She laughs.

The demonstration had been forbidden by the prefect of Paris, and the government had seized *L'Humanité*. The police shot at the demonstrators at Place de Stalingrad. Hocine Belaïd, a municipal employee in Aubervilliers, a Communist militant and immigrant from Algeria, was shot and died of his wounds a few hours later. A few blocks away, the head of the Communist Party was arrested with a gun in his car. It was a time of unbridled state violence and active class war.

Lucie explains that when the first people moved into the *cité* at the beginning of the 1960s, they did not know the ring road would be built there, passing right by their windows and splitting the social housing complex in two. At the time, three buildings were on Paris's side, while a fourth one was just outside the Zone, then an open space where children liked to play.

Aerial photograph from 1962 featuring the Cité des Fougères.

When construction started, the residents chatted with the workers and the engineers supervising the works. The workers warned them: 'If you live on the first floors you won't feel it as much, but the higher you are, the noisier it's going to be.' On 1 December 1969, the section of the ring road that went by Lucie's flat opened to traffic. On that day, permanent commotion settled in and life in the Cité des Fougères became unbearable. Inhabitants sought peace by sleeping in their bathtubs and corridors, far away from the windows. The local GP started prescribing antidepressants and sleeping pills, while children mourned the immense playground they had lost. 'As soon as the ring road arrived, we started fighting to have it covered.' The people of the *cité* were on the warpath with a behemoth: the Parisian technocracy.

By its physical magnitude, by the time spent on its construction – two decades – by its place in the landscape, the ring road is the most important piece of infrastructure to be built in Paris in the second half of the twentieth century. And yet it does not have a creator incarnate: a single architect, an engineer or a mayor that built a legacy from its creation. Its construction has not been documented, it does not feature in coffee-table architecture books, its anniversaries are not celebrated. The ring road of Paris is the city's most gargantuan and invisible monument.

It was a collective effort. Imagined by Vichy (1940–4), voted by the Fourth (1946–58) but built by the Fifth Republic (1958), the ring road is the brainchild of three regimes and one ideology: French technocracy. This faceless ensemble of civil servants personifying – and self-identifying as – France's elite designed a highly efficient but immensely disruptive piece of infrastructure that remains a burden in the construction of Parisian identity. Made of ink and administrative correspondence as much as concrete and steel rods, the ring road is the result of a complex design process that apprehended the city of Paris as an abstract, highly malleable matter, with little consideration for the physical ordeal endured by its neighbours, like Lucie Lapuszanska.

Yet Paris planners did not design in a vacuum. They considered their *grande oeuvre* as a cultural and political endeavour that might reshape Paris's visage for the century to come. It was about motor traffic, of course, but was mostly considered an urban planning project that would be the catalyst for a renovation of the banlieue. Just as René Mestais had envisioned it in 1943. Its reception echoed the promise and disappointments of modernism and modernity – Parisians loved it when they saw renders in magazines and models in exhibitions, then loathed it when it passed by their windows.

The production of the Boulevard Périphérique was also one of power, money and influence. While the little people vainly petitioned and demonstrated, the rich and powerful met discreetly in salons to obtain detours and coverings of the ring road by their homes. By opening the black box of design entanglements that make up the Boulevard Périphérique, I will tell you how the journey to create a highly technical, 'apolitical' infrastructure led to moral corruption and social bias. I will tell you how the bourgeois defended their privilege, and how technocracy shaped the space of Paris to their image.

Technocracy can be described as the government of a society by an elite of technical experts that privilege a 'rational' and 'scientific' administration over democratic legitimacy. The term was coined in the first half of the twentieth century in the United States, where a technocracy movement – Technocracy Inc. – was created in the 1930s, then exported to France after World War II. Yet the idea of technocracy predated the coining of the word and is rooted more profoundly in the French imagination.

For the historian Antoine Picon, the eighteenth century marked the emergence of a French technocratic ideal when engineers moved away from their military roots to found civil corps, while the principles of Enlightenment established a relation between material and moral progress.[1] A Corps des ponts et chaussées (Corps for Bridges and Roads) and a Corps des mines (Corps for Mining) were created, and with them prestigious, highly selective schools to train engineers. In these schools, students not only learned technical design, mathematics and physics but also shared codes and practice. These men – women were allowed starting only in the 1970s – went through rites of passage and developed a camaraderie that bound them for the rest of their lives, creating a social group, a community, an elite. Some have changed names, but these corps and their schools remain in place today. They pursue the same mission: shaping France by moulding its elite. And as is evidenced by the continued use of the term 'corps', the martial culture of engineering – the idea of a collective, a band of brothers – survived as the field passed from the military into the civil sphere.

Another key figure of French technocratic culture was Henri de Rouvroy de Saint-Simon – whom I have briefly mentioned already – and the posthumous utopian movement he inspired. A complex intellectual movement born in the first half of the nineteenth century, Saint-Simonianism rested on the belief that technological progress would change society for the better, bringing happiness, emancipation and freedom.

After Saint-Simon's death, the movement split into different sects – including an influential church led by Prosper Enfantin, where disciples wore a uniform that had buttons only in the back, so they always needed someone's help to dress, as a reminder that an individual is nothing without a supporting community – that promoted varied readings of Saint-Simon's philosophy. Saint-Simonianism is commonly identified as a form of utopian socialism, and Karl Marx and Friedrich Engels considered Saint-Simon one of the most influential intellectuals of socialism. Yet somehow confusingly (from our contemporary point of view), the Count de Saint-Simon was also the flagship thinker for proponents of free trade and capitalism. His philosophy inspired the great capitalists of the nineteenth century to invest in railway companies in order to reach new markets and connect humanity by way of technology and trade.

The French technocratic movement gathered momentum in the 1930s. At École Polytechnique, France's most prestigious engineering school, which is also a military school, a group of engineers and economists created the think tank X-Crise – 'X' being the nickname of the school, and 'crise' referring to the global financial crisis of 1929 and its aftermath. The political ideologies represented in the group ranged from economic liberalism to socialism, but the collective agreed on politicians' inability to take pertinent decisions regarding economics and technical planning. When the group dissolved in 1940, its members split between those who joined the Resistance, those who became active collaborators and those who pursued careers in Occupied France without actively choosing a side and therefore ended up working as civil servants for the Vichy regime.

In the first months of its establishment, the Vichy regime was perceived by some French social elites (including engineers and civil servants) as a long-hoped-for opportunity to fix the issues that a drowsy Third Republic could not address, impeded by the weight of parliamentarianism. To put it bluntly, for these men France was rid of democracy and its old ideological frameworks, now ready for a new type of pure technocratic regime that Pétain's ideology – the National Revolution – would serve.

In 1940, regime supporters created the National Executive Youth School of Uriage, which was attended by aspiring technocrats eager to modernise the French State. The story of this school offers a good illustration of the Vichy regime's infatuation with technocrats and their complex unfolding relationship. As the regime furthered its collaboration with the German Third Reich, some of Uriage's educators and students interpreted the principles taught in the school as a call to join the Resistance, while others understood them as an inspiration to remain faithful to the autocratic government of Marshal Pétain.

The school was dissolved in 1943 by Prime Minister Pierre Laval. The school's director, General Pierre Dunoyer de Segonzac, joined the Resistance. After the war, as another testament to Vichy's complex and ambivalent relationship to postwar urbanism, some of Uriage's students became key figures of urbanism – for example, one of the founders of urban sociology in France, Paul-Henry Chombart de Lauwe, and the top civil servant that ruled over Paris for a quarter of a century (a character we met in the previous chapter): Paul Delouvrier.

In 1958, French technocracy reached its climax with General de Gaulle's return to power and the design of a new constitution to serve his ambitions. Just like the Third, the Fourth Republic, established in 1946, was a parliamentary regime, meaning the legislative chambers led the political game. The people elected the members of parliament who then elected a prime minister in charge of leading the country, and a head of state, whose role was mainly cosmetic. If the MPs were displeased with the prime minister and their government, they deposed him. The constitutional design of the Fourth Republic and the French political landscape resulted in significant political instability: twenty-four governments in twelve years. The political situation degraded rapidly in 1957 and 1958 as the Algerian War of Independence – described at the time as 'events' – evolved into a full-blown conflict that shook up French society and led to the Fifth Republic in 1958.

From a parliamentary regime, the Fifth Republic would be a semi-presidential regime, in which a president of the Republic existed alongside a prime minister. In theory, the prime minister was in charge. In practice though, the president led the country, while the prime minister obeyed – and this remains the case today. When a political situation turns sour, the president fires the prime minister, out of self-interest. And so the president governs, unchallenged, while the prime minister takes the blow.

And at the very top of the pyramid, incarnating the new republic's culture of leadership, the six-foot, five-inch towering figure of the *général*. De Gaulle's ideology as he returned to power was essentially anti-parliamentarian: no more lengthy discussions and consensus-seeking – the decisions would be made at the top and implemented with little room for contestation. Modern and 'forward-thinking', de Gaulle's France rested on a strong public administration, on the country's technical and administrative elites.

Among the policies that needed swift progress was the reorganisation of an unruly and rebellious array of cities: Paris and the banlieue. The capital city was an obvious and easy target to unleash all the dreams of modern technocratic planning, for it was devoid of any local leader that could resist the Fifth Republic's administration. Indeed, Paris, since the Commune of 1871, had been forbidden to elect a mayor.

On 14 July 1789, Jacques de Flesselles was shot dead in front of Paris City Hall. His head was then severed, put on a pike and paraded by the mob that had stormed the Bastille Fortress just a few hours before and then served the same treatment to its governor, Marquis de Launay. Etymologically, a marquis is a nobleman defending the *marche* of the kingdom, an archaic name for 'frontier'. Here, the frontier was that of Paris and banlieue, as the loathed Bastille castle was both a prison and an element of the medieval wall that bounded the city.

De Flesselles was the last provost of the merchants of Paris, a function roughly equivalent to London's lord mayor. Elected by the bourgeois of Paris for terms of two years, the provost was in charge of the city's administration, urban planning and tax collection. The day after his murder, Jean Sylvain Bailly, a mathematician and astronomer, was appointed with a new title: mayor of Paris. Guillotined in 1793, Bailly's initial term had been followed by a series of short-lived mandates – and cut-short mayors – until the final appointment of Jean-Baptiste Fleuriot-Lescot. He remained in post for two months before he was also arrested for supporting Robespierre and for his attempt to lead the Parisians in revolt. He was guillotined alongside his mentor the day after his arrest, on 28 July 1794.

After Fleuriot-Lescot's bid to spark a revolt by the Parisians, the First Republic decided to cancel the mayorship of Paris. The idea of the country's most defiant people, the Parisians, electing a leader in the capital city, where all the country's top institutions – executive, legislative, judiciary – were located, was considered too threatening for the state. This defiance is a key element to understanding the way the municipal institutions of Paris were organised in the nineteenth century and well into the twentieth: the central state was *afraid* of Paris.[2] Paris was then put under the tutelage of the state and local democracy suspended.

After the revolution of 1848, the Second Republic was proclaimed and the function of mayor of Paris was reinstated in February, only to be abolished again in July following the insurrection of June 1848. Then came the revolution of 1870, the fall of Napoleon III and the appointment by acclamation of a mayor for Paris, Étienne Arago. He was replaced two months later by Jules Ferry who fled the city on the first day of the Paris Commune, to join Adolphe Thiers. After the Commune of Paris, the function of mayor was abolished for the third time since its creation in 1789. This last cancellation would hold for more than one hundred years.

Despite all the regime change, despite all the progress of liberalism and democracy, the tutelage went on. Indeed, while Paris was ruled by its tutor, the governance of other cities followed the changes of time and the evolution of political philosophy. The law of 1867 had given more power to cities and their aediles, while the one of April 1884 had enacted the democratic election – not open to women voters or candidates – of the mayors and the municipal council. But none of these essential laws applied to Paris, where the council and its president – who was not allowed to be called *maire* – had but a superficial role. Nothing changed with the instauration of the Fourth Republic in 1946 and then the Fifth Republic in 1958. Paris was still forbidden to elect a mayor.

It was only in the 1970s, after decades of lobbying that the governance of Paris would change significantly with the law no. 75-1331 of December 1975, which reinstated a mayor for the first time since the Commune. In March 1977, following the first universal election of its history, the conservative candidate Jacques Chirac was elected. The state had finally suspended its tutelage of the capital city, 183 years after it was implemented. The ring road had been inaugurated four years before.

Until 1977, Paris was therefore governed by two civil servants, two prefects in charge of carrying out the state's tutelage. The prefect for the Seine, the name of the administrative entity that included Paris and extended into the banlieue, was in charge of urban planning, public transport, housing, education and so on. The prefect of police for Paris was specifically in charge of policing the population – control, repression, management of demonstrations and surveillance. This duo of prefects did not exist in any other city in France.

Each town in the banlieue, on the other hand, had mayors – in charge of urban planning, for instance, or allowing building permits – but they still had to deal with the prefect of the Seine, who retained some form of control over their policy. The prefect of the Seine was, therefore, the executive head of Paris and the civil servant in charge of overseeing development in the rest of the *préfecture*, including all the adjacent suburban towns. When de Gaulle seized power in 1958, and designed the institutions of the Fifth Republic, Paris already offered the dream of a technocratic government with civil servants at its head and virtually no democratic local counterpowers. The new ideology in place at the national level would only strengthen that momentum.

Infrastructure like the ring road is made of administrative correspondence as much as engineers' drawings and designs. Sometimes the two are mixed, almost literally – for instance, when the maintenance workers of the city found boxes of paper in a pile on the ring road a few years back, half-eaten by rats and covered in rodents' urine, with blueprints, calculations, reports and photographs. In my own time, I have rummaged through hundreds of those boxes because I wanted to understand how the Boulevard Périphérique was designed.

Why does it snake discreetly underground in some sections, while it is elevated as a viaduct in others? Why does it bend here, straighten there? Who checked the engineers' calculations? Who made decisions? In essence, I wanted to understand how technocracy plans infrastructure like the ring road, and to unearth the political, cultural and ethno-racial biases that necessarily made up these technocrats' minds.

The way civil servants send their paperwork to be archived is very strict. By law, they are not allowed to destroy any physical or digital document they have produced in the course of their professional duties without an express authorisation granted by the head of the archives. Once filed to be archived – for instance, when a case is closed, or a civil servant retires – these archives are protected by a twenty-five-year gag order. It extends to fifty years if the file encloses any kind of personal data. Of course, not all documents are kept – for instance, if they are deemed to be of little historical value. Some documents are also lost or destroyed by mistake. Finally, we cannot avoid imagining that some compromising documents are purposely left out or removed from the archives, even if it means breaking the law.

In the years the ring road was designed, exchanges were all on paper. By opening the boxes stored in the Archives de Paris – housed in a fascinating 1990 PoMo building leaning against the ring road – and reading the piles of paper they store, we can follow the journey of an issue at all stages of its discussion. We have access to the *crafting* of a decision. Fifty years on, by reading draft after draft of an issue going up and down the hierarchy, we witness how technocracy – not an anonymous mass anymore, but a group of individuals with names, characters, ambitions, mannerisms, distinct handwriting – worked to shape the urban planning decisions of Paris.

Two *portes* of Paris, two sections of the ring road, illustrate the way politics is embedded in its design. One is Porte de Ménilmontant, where Lucie lives. The other is Porte de Champerret, south of the seventeenth arrondissement, as it connects to the affluent sixteenth arrondissement. Ménilmontant was and remains a working-class area, represented by Communist and socialist councillors. Porte de

Champerret on the other hand, like most of the west of Paris, is among the city's wealthiest neighbourhoods and represented by conservative councillors. The opposed social biases at play offer a window into the kind of technocratic city-making processes that continue to shape the landscape of Paris today.

At first unaware that the ring road was going to be built by their windows, the inhabitants at Porte de Ménilmontant reacted swiftly when they realised what was going to hit them. In 1967, their local councillors took their case to heart and put through a bill to the municipal council to have the ring road covered – which entailed adding a roof on the motorway that runs through open trench so that it becomes a tunnel, while de facto creating an empty area above to plant gardens, build play grounds or erect light structures . Without much discussion, the resolution was approved by political parties across the chamber and forwarded to the prefect to be implemented. Two years later, on 1 December 1969, the section of the ring road by Lucie's windows opened.

Today, an urban motorway is a familiar artefact. They are everywhere in cities across the globe. But at the end of the 1960s, motorways were a rare sight, in Europe at least, and cities' high-speed thoroughfares were a novel type of communication infrastructure. So imagine when a barrier was lifted in the wee hours of 1 December 1969 and suddenly hundreds of cars revved down the access roads to take a go at this brand-new stretch of macadam. The space that was an endless green playground for children just a few years before became a circuit for middle-class men in their carcasses of metal, spewing toxic fumes.

Meanwhile, the cover that the municipal council voted on was nowhere to be seen. The prefect's engineers had simply ignored the councillors' decision. The councillors did not receive a rebuttal from the department for roads, or a frank *non*: the democratically elected representatives of the Parisian people were given the cold shoulder of technocracy, plain and simple. In 1960s Paris, technocrats were so powerful they did not even need to play the game of democracy. When a decision did not meet their focus, they moved on. The inhabitants petitioned, demonstrated, lobbied. The councillors made speeches, addresses, bills, votes, formal protests. But the administration refused to budge. For years, they ignored the thousands of households, choked by air pollution, driven mad by the noise of motor traffic, gulping down cocktails of drugs, that asked for help.

Inhabitants at Porte de Ménilmontant were not alone in their predicament: at Porte de Vanves, Porte Pouchet, Porte de Clignancourt – all social housing in working-class neighbourhoods – the ring road lay just a few metres from residents' windows. All were united in their suffering, but all were ignored by the Department for Roads. The arguments they received in reply to their many letters were always the same. First, the Department for Roads would tell the petitioners that it was the Office for Affordable Housing of Paris that built their homes too close to the projected ring road, despite being aware of its upcoming construction. Second, they systematically denied the reality of inhabitants' ordeals. Reading these letters describing the daily hardship of the ring road's neighbours, and the cold, technical replies they received, we find ourselves faced with two sets of thoughts, two points of view.

On the one hand, consider the inhabitants. They did not fundamentally oppose the ring road: they also owned or aspired to own cars; they embraced car culture. For instance, at Porte de Vanves residents suggested covering the ring road there and making this new slab of concrete above the motorway an open-air car park – not exactly a radical anti-car positioning. But they also suffered from the negative externality of the ring road: the noise and the 'toxic fumes' from car exhaust – two elements that were not yet called 'pollution'. Their fantasy of the gleaming road had crashed against the stark reality of its everyday hostility, its stench, its bedlam.

The city's engineers, on the other hand, collectively maintained that fantasy – building roads was, after all, their livelihood. I think they loved what they designed; they were proud of it: a modern, highly efficient piece of infrastructure. But I have never found evidence that these engineers lived a few metres from it. Their answers to petitions considered the issue from a technical point of view. Noise, they would reply, was a necessary outcome of car traffic. The road was in perfect condition – no potholes, the most modern coating, and the elevation limited to avoid motors roaring and brakes screeching as cars and lorries went up and downhill. Solace would not come from the road itself, they argued in a letter, but from quieter cars and thicker apartment windows – even if, as a handwritten note left on that same letter acknowledged, the latter solution would make homes unbearable in the summer.

Though the engineers of the Department for Roads rejected the idea that noise from road traffic was an issue and denied that their design could have taken this element into account, urban din was not a 'new' topic at the time. It was a well-established social problem. While it is notoriously difficult to scientifically evaluate whether a period in history was 'noisier' than previous ones, we can at least analyse the increased sensitivity to specific sounds and their cultural meanings at specific times. The postwar opinion of technocrats, scientists, acousticians and musicians did revolve around the belief that the world had never been so noisy, and that (mechanical) noise had become a threat to human health.

Several books were published on this topic in France in the 1950s and 1960s; the Ministry for Public Health, the Academy of Medicine, professional bodies and lobbies had working groups dedicated to the 'plague' of noise in the city. The creator of the influential League Against Noise, a doctor and hygienist named Fernand Trémolières, had written a notable book in 1955 on this topic, with a foreword by none other than Bernard Lafay, the politician who so vehemently defended the ring road that now deafened its neighbours. We can still read today in the archives of the Department for Roads their anno-tated synthesis of the discussions. Noise in the city, and specifically noise from car traffic, was an omnipresent topic that engineers of the Paris administration did not ignore. Yet throughout the 1960s and 1970s, as sections of the ring road opened, as neighbours complained, as depressive and anxious states became widespread, technocrats refused to publicly acknowledge the reality of sonic pollution.

A letter I dug up from the archives reveals quite bluntly the strat-egy behind the Department for Roads' position. It refers to the future trials of sound walls on the ring road. A common sight today, they were at the time a new technology, and Parisian engineers were not enthralled. 'To carry out this trial on the ring road is already admit-ting that the infrastructure creates an unacceptable nuisance, since the City of Paris is trying to find a remedy', explains the engineer to his boss, in an effort to discourage him from the plan. The engineer continues:

> If the trial is successful we will have to equip the ring road in its quasi-totality, and if the trial is unsuccessful we will find ourselves dealing with a series of complaints regarding our incapacity to propose a solution to the evident problems created by the road's presence (since we have tried to provide a remedy).

The engineer's position is clear: by trying to mitigate against noise with a trial run of sound walls – whether that trial be successful or not – they would be acknowledging publicly that noise is an issue and would end up bearing its burden. The trial was sabotaged by the engineers. It was never carried out, and Paris technocracy continued to ignore the issue of noise.

While the inhabitants of Cité des Fougères used all the tools of democracy available to them to have their voices heard, another negotiation took place about covering the ring road, this time on the other side of the city, by Porte de Champerret.

On 9 Rue Catulle Mendès lived Henri P. A graduate of the Arts et Métiers and Centrale – two prestigious Parisian engineering schools – he was also the son of a famous French engineer who created a company he named after himself. Henri P. worked as a consultant for the Ministry for Construction and was one of the experts commissioned by the court to give his professional view on the accident of Boulevard Lefebvre, an HLM of the City of Paris that collapsed on 15 January 1964 during construction, killing twenty workers. At the end of the 1960s, Henri P. was, therefore, a well-connected, influential engineer, who was not only an heir to his father but also a trusted expert in his own right.

The elegant building where he lived, which still exists today, stands about fifty metres from the ring road. When Henri P. wrote his first letters to the administration of Paris, his flat still faced the empty Zone, but the construction of the Boulevard Périphérique was ineluctable – it was a matter of years, months maybe. A well-travelled engineer, P. seemed to have been more aware of the risks that having a high-speed road pass by his home entailed. He was also possibly worried that the Boulevard Périphérique might devalue his property.

And so, Henri P. mobilised his networks, his social skills and his technical knowledge to lobby the Parisian technocracy. And we can follow his journey, letter after letter.

P. knew the arcane of Paris's technocracy and which doors to knock on. Through correspondence and meetings with the head of urban planning and the director for road design, P. submitted new blueprints for the ring road. His idea was simple: the road could swerve away from his home to go deeper into the banlieue. In doing so, it would be making room for a large green space between his building and the road. The letters and the plans he sent are all kept in the archives. His move was cocky and cleverly delivered, with the perfect balance of obsequiousness and borderline bullying. And yet despite his insistence, his request was denied and the case was closed. Officially.

Upon reading P.'s request, which had been formally denied, I remembered that a few months prior I had read another dossier on that very *porte*, the one where P. lived. I went through my notes, returned to the archives and opened the box that I had previously consulted without taking much notice of its content. The debate among engineers had a slightly different focus. It was not about changing the route of the ring road to move away from the homes of wealthy Parisians and cutting through the facing banlieue, but about building a cover right in front of . . . 9 Rue Catulle Mendès, P.'s home address.

The roof atop the ring road running in open trench there would be incomplete, but, according to the designers, it would be enough to protect the building from the noise, and trees would be planted on it too, so that it would blend into the landscape. Upon receiving the initial proposal by the engineer in charge of the case, the head of urban planning, André Herzog – who personally reviewed the design

– asked specifically that a new perspective be drawn, one that illustrated clearly that no cars driving on the ring road would be visible from the top of 9 Rue Catulle Mendès.

The case does not mention Henri P.'s name. The folder kept in the archives presents the major design intervention as the Department for Roads' own initiative. But one telling detail gives it up. Between the letters and the blueprints, I found Henri P.'s calling card, with a date handwritten on it. That date might refer to a meeting or a phone call. What this calling card reveals is that Henri P. was actively involved in updating the design of the ring road in front of his home and that he had, in the end, succeeded.

It took Henri P. a few letters, a handful of meetings, a fair amount of social skill and his wide-ranging network to obtain a major change to the way the ring road was to be designed as it snaked by his home. The whole process lasted a year or so. East of the city, by the time the residents of Cité des Fougères at long last obtained the cover of the ring road by their homes in 1975, eight years had passed – including six with the ring road in full activity.

The thousands of working-class residents and the councillors representing them had fought with the tools of democracy. They got what they wanted, eventually, but not because of the strength of their arguments or the vehemence of their protests, but because of a change of national policy. In 1971, France created for the first time a Ministry for the Environment. Pollution had become a political issue acknowledged at the highest level. In typical top-down technocratic fashion, the issue trickled down from the prime minister to the prefects, and then to the Paris administration which – without entirely acknowledging its mistakes – had to start taking action, if reluctantly.

The two covers at Porte de Champerret and Porte de Ménilmontant had the same financial cost for the city, but one was carried out slowly and begrudgingly despite its urgency, and the other was negotiated in elegant city hall offices and parqueted mens' clubs and delivered swiftly, almost as a courtesy — an urbane gesture from one member of the elite to another.

The French like their republican king, the *président*. Not that they like the individual specifically — his or her politics or character — but they enjoy having the figure of a monarch. Even when the president is loathed, they *love* loathing the guy. As for all other politicians, the further in the past they were in office, the smoother and happier the memories are. Charles de Gaulle is now often described in hagiographic terms: a charismatic, no-bullshit figure, a war hero who was close to the people, despised money and disdained the powerful, was pious but not devout, was faithful to his friends and his values, a visionary, a strategist. And like all the monarchs of the Fifth Republic, de Gaulle got drawn into architecture and urban planning — specifically Paris's. Reshaping the city for the centuries to come is the privilege of kings. It is the ultimate power, the noble mark one leaves in history.

Traditionally, French presidents have left one significant architecture project as their legacy. Jacques Chirac created the Musée du Quai Branly, designed by Jean Nouvel and that ended up bearing the president's name . François Mitterrand was very active on that front in his fourteen years of presidency and has left many architectural imprints on the city, including the Great Arch of the Défense, Paris's business district, and the Louvre Pyramid designed by I. M. Pei. The pyramid and the arch are on each extremity of a perspective known as the *royal way*, including the Champs-Élysées. Mitterrand's legacy is, therefore, the remodelling of Paris's most ancient and prestigious axis.

Charles de Gaulle's heritage is at the same time more subtle and more profound, and consists in the entire reshaping of Paris street hardware and reorganisation of the city's infrastructure – from the ring road to the RER, the regional transport system for Paris; from Paris's airports to the relocation of the city's principal food markets from the Halles district to Rungis; from the creation of nine New Towns outside Paris to the complete overhaul of Paris and its regional urban planning administration. Each major planning decision had to go by him, and just as Mitterrand reviewed stone samples for the cladding of the Great Arch of the Défense, de Gaulle reviewed designs and eventually made his choice, alone.

An anecdote, partly legend, has it that he once passed through one of the Elysée Palace's salons where a model maker was setting up the miniatures for the Halles district architectural competition, a day before the meeting where the relevant officials would have explained all the projects on display. De Gaulle derailed his minuted schedule and asked the model maker to explain each of the projects that his workshops had realised; he asked him his opinion and then made his own up on the spot. This story feeds into the legend of no-bullshit, close-to-the-people de Gaulle, and has – like all legends – some nuggets of truth in it.

Since the beginning of the 1960s, a section of the ring road had been particularly disputed. All other parts of the Boulevard Périphérique were either being built or already delivered, but the debate on the section from Porte de Saint-Cloud to Porte Maillot was still raging. West of Paris, this section goes between the wealthy sixteenth arrondissement and the Bois de Boulogne, one of Paris's two parks, along with the Bois de Vincennes.

The Bois de Boulogne that today houses the Fondation Louis Vuitton is next to Paris's most privileged neighbourhoods and adjacent to equally rich suburban towns. The *bois* is the archetypal space of the Parisian establishment. No other section of the urban motorway has ever been so fiercely debated: the municipal council engaged with the topic of the ring road's design in this area several times, and at length. Meanwhile, we see in the archives of the Department for Roads the intense lobbying from Paris's elites to obtain the rerouting or the plain annulment of this section of the ring road. MPs, ministers and councillors wrote to the prefect insistently to ask for information and favours, and to complain that they were being constantly harassed by their constituents.

Logically, the ring road there would have had to go in a straight line between the Bois de Boulogne and the city, through the Allée des Fortifications. This was the original design that had been envisioned since the late 1950s. But in a strange turn of events, the engineers suddenly realised that a water pipe prevented them from completing the project. In the grand scheme of things, that a water pipe would justify the rerouting of an entire section of the Boulevard Périphérique seems unlikely. Despite the suspicion expressed by the councillors in the opposition who denounced the great difference in attitude towards the residents of sixteenth arrondissement, whose right to tranquillity was treated with utmost respect, and those in working-class areas that saw the ring road literally coming up in front of their windows, the municipal council approved the design proposed by the administration.

The new design would cut through the *bois* underground and avoid disturbing the activities of the Auteuil racecourse, one of the super-rich of Paris's favourite hobbies. The ring road would make a slight detour but would be cheaper to build according to the engineers – despite the large underground sections – and, astonishingly, would lead to less uprooting of trees, despite going right through the park of Boulogne.

The building works were about to start when Charles de Gaulle stepped in and put a halt to it. The prefect sent a letter to the engineers of the Department for Roads and asked for an immediate pause. The route of the ring road would be the subject of a dedicated Restricted Council by May of the same year. A *Conseil restreint* is a high-level meeting chaired by the president of the Republic that involves the prime minister, relevant ministers and top civil servants (or high-ranking army officers). Such events should have been limited to traditional presidential domains (such as matters of defence, colonial wars, international trade and so on) but as de Gaulle limited the influence of his prime ministers, he also increased the number of Restricted Councils he would hold, and the scope of the issues discussed by him directly.

And de Gaulle decided the route of the Boulevard Périphérique in the Bois de Boulogne was too sensitive to be left to the Council of Paris and the prefect. Or it might be that he was already unsatisfied with the route and set on changing it. Some say de Gaulle had not liked the media's assumption that the rich and powerful had had their way and rerouted the ring road for their convenience. 'Isn't it that we don't want the ring road to go in front of the windows of Mr Dassault?' de Gaulle candidly asked his staff, referring to a rich and powerful industrialist and politician. 'This is precisely why the Boulevard Périphérique should pass there.' Other sources tell that de Gaulle got involved because his secretary general did his jogging in the Bois de Boulogne and brought up the topic with the president. One thing is certain: the involvement of de Gaulle was the direct result of the neighbourhood sociology (and that of the president's entourage). We can safely assume that not many technical advisors to de Gaulle or powerful CEOs lived at Porte de Clignancourt, Porte de Vanves or Porte de Ménilmontant.

Was it all a stunt? Was de Gaulle's wrath political propaganda meant to demonstrate that the presidency did not leave accusations of corruption and favouritism unchallenged? We will never know the answer – the minutes of the meeting, unlike other councils of this nature, have not been kept in the archives, although it is unlikely there was not a secretary to type them up, considering the high-level nature of the discussion. The actual words spoken that day will remain mysterious, but in a final twist, de Gaulle eventually followed his prefect's opinion on the Bois de Boulogne and did not manage, or did not want, to counter the decisions taken by the prefect and his administration. To save a racetrack and preserve the quality of life of the wealthy residents of the *bois*, the ring road had to make a detour – de Gaulle, his government and the Paris administration all agreed, as gentlemen.

Past 8 p.m. on the 25 May 2022: the Porte de Champerret is crowded and the Boulevard Périphérique clogged. The evening is heavy and humid; it will rain in a moment. I had to take a phone call that could not wait, I am listening and talking while walking around a three-by-six-metre street vent that services the covered section of the ring road beneath my feet. A young man arrives riding his kick scooter, with two weighty-looking plastic shopping bags dangling on his handlebars. He gets off his ride and glances at me before jumping the fence that forbids pedestrians to get any closer to the road. He is swallowed by the sad looking but dense vegetation that grows on the exterior embankments of the Périphérique.

Where is he walking to, I wonder, a secret drinking spot? A tent where he lives? His stash? I hang up the phone and gaze at this uncanny infrastructure landscape. The ring road is thrumming, with its four lanes going clockwise, and four lanes going counterclockwise. On my left stands the partial cover negotiated by Henri P. to protect his home from the impact of the ring road. I look at the windows of the top flat of 9 Rue Catulle Mendès, and I wonder whether his descendants still live there, whether the story of *grand-papa* Henri convincing the prefect to cover the ring road in front of the family apartment is one they proudly tell every Christmas at dinner.

On my right is the entry gate to Promenade Bernard Lafay. The walk is a grim green space that winds behind a 'sonic hill' – this is the technical term to describe it – designed to shield the noise of traffic from the flaneurs and the users of the nursery and professional school built here. On top of noise pollution, the children, residents and professionals living and working here daily are the recipients of increased amounts of harmful particulate matter ($PM_{2.5}$, PM_{10}), nitric oxides (NO) and nitrogen dioxides (NO_2) compared to the rest of Paris. Indeed, the immediate proximity of the ring road has taken its toll on the elongated park and the buildings: the dirt and the yellowish, sickly vegetation are the familiar signs of the Boulevard Périphérique's impact on its immediate surroundings.

The Bois de Boulogne is not far. I picture the ring road that elegantly moves away from the residential buildings by the Allée des Fortifications to discreetly plunge under the large park, leaving undisturbed the posh flats and the Auteuil racetrack. I think about the thousands of people evicted from their homes on the Zone, of the houses taken down in working-class suburbs to build the ring road. You would like more subtlety, more contrast, but the ring road is almost a caricature of the classic power struggles between the rich and powerful on the one side, and the poor and vulnerable on the other.

In his book *Artifice and Design*, the philosopher Barry Allen questions technology's fantasised 'pure' nature. There is no 'one best way' to design an artefact, he argues, even a highly technical one like a bridge. Allen calls this the 'fallacy of functionality', our assumption that if a technological artefact – like a ring road – is designed in the way it has been designed, it is purely to maximise efficiency. This is probably how an engineer working for the Department for Roads then (and now) would have earnestly replied. The ring road was designed in this way because this was the only and best way, as per the rules of engineering. But a technology is always social, because

> what 'works' is conditioned as much by available or invented technology as by the political, economic, historical, and aesthetic contexts that ultimately define any 'technological' problem, as well as the scope of acceptable solutions.[3]

The ring road is often presented as a non-subject: it looks like that because it was put on the 'empty' Zone and was designed by an apolitical, technocratic regime with engineering as its only book of law. But the ring road is an architecture of power, the crystallisation of the social biases that structure French society and its hierarchy of classes. Sometimes these social biases are buried beneath so many layers of 'technical' design that one forgets they ever existed: this detour gets justified by the number of trees it will save instead of the residents' flats it will spare, this bend that has led to dozens of homes being destroyed in the banlieue is explained by the demands of increased security for car drivers. That an engineer with strong Catholic beliefs has proposed this design to save a church from being destroyed – a story I will save for another time – gets forgotten entirely. The ring road is a technological, and therefore, intrinsically social and political artefact.

The nitty-gritty of its design reveals that even an almost perfect technocratic government, as Paris was at the time, did not improve efficiency or rational planning. Indeed, the Boulevard Périphérique is an impressive feat: thirty-six kilometres of road built in a dense urban setting over less than two decades. But the technocratic management of this process only added opacity, without improving the fairness of its design for the community of Parisians and *banlieusards* at large.

The technocratic elite that built the road did not design it in a vacuum – they, too, were influenced by status, fame, power and connections. They got corrupted, to a certain extent. Not by taking bribes, but by serving the elites they belonged to not necessarily by birth, by studying hard, graduating from the top engineering schools in the country and being appointed to France's most prestigious positions in civil service. The Parisian technocrats believed in other technocrats, they believed in elitism, instead of using their power to plan a fairer city.

The lessons we take away from studying how the ring road was designed remain valid to this day. The myth of technocracy remains strong in France, in Europe. The fantasy that an elite group of civil servants, politicians, businesspeople and technologists, knows best. And that freed from the burden of democracy they will excel, building a fairer society for the many and not the few – not for themselves, that is. The two terms of Emmanuel Macron, himself trained in the country's most prestigious civil service school, have tapped into that imaginary. In October 2017, the president referred to the *premiers de cordée*, the lead climbers, to describe the necessity to have an elite dragging the rest of the country's plebs in its wake.

In March 1977, Jacques Chirac was elected mayor of Paris. Among the key issues he vowed to tackle in his campaign was the nuisance of the ring road, completed just a few years prior. Paris had tipped into a new political regime, democracy, and the voices of the people now demanded to be heard – if only for Chirac to stand a chance at being reelected six years later. The Department for Roads that had resolutely opposed any design intervention in connection to noise, justifying their position with 'technical' arguments (the sound wall will fail) as well as aesthetic ones (it will be ugly, and therefore unacceptable), had no choice but to operate a complete overhaul of their position. They were civil servants, and their new boss, the mayor, would not take it. The same engineers who had rejected noise-proofing designs just a few years before would now implement them. Technology itself had not changed over those years, but 'technical reason' had to embrace a new political and social mindset.

5

Rust Belt, White City: Colonial Paris and the Margins of the Empire

Forests charm and ravish us as much as they inspire fear and caution. When the sun hides and turns the crooked trees into anxious ghosts, when the leaves in the wind morph from sonic glitter to fairyhood gloom, I shudder. Even the most urbane coppices hold within them the ancient fears of wild beasts, loneliness and fear for one's soul. On this cool, sunny July morning, cycling through the inviting, familiar, friendly Bois de Vincennes, a large wood east of Paris, a sense of gloom and sadness takes hold of me, one that I should have anticipated. There are ghosts here, hidden in the ruins I have come to visit.

I reach my destination: the Garden for Tropical Agronomy, formerly known as the Colonial Trial Garden. A fake 'Chinese gate', built over a century ago, welcomes the visitor who enters this discreet park, unbeknownst to Parisians and tourists. A plump cat watches over the empty main alley. At the table of the *jardin*'s charity-run café, a woman is sitting wearing – you could not make it up – a white hat shaped like a pith helmet, the traditional colonial headgear. The gleaming white walls of the Tunisia pavilion, recently refurbished, dazzle as the sun comes out from behind the clouds.

Hidden around the garden are queer pavilions inspired by vernacular architectures of the colonies – or reinterpretations of them based on European fantasies. Most have fallen into ruins, left to be devoured by the relentless vegetation, which includes species from all around the fallen French empire, brought here at the end of the nineteenth century.

On this site, in 1907, a colonial exhibition was held. One of many that took place then – in Paris, London and Brussels. Pavilions displayed six recreated 'villages': Congolese, Indochinese, Kanak, Malagasy, Sudanese and Tuareg. Human zoos. Where white men with fedoras, suits and walking canes came on Sundays to drool in front of the naked breasts of the women in the Congolese village, where white women in long elegant dresses borrowed Tuareg babies from their mothers to play with in the recreated campsite. Two million visitors came to the quiet suburb of Nogent-sur-Marne in 1907 to see the 'savages' of the colonies in their 'primitive' state.

The ghosts of Vincennes have come from Morocco, Vietnam, Algeria, Benin, Sudan, Kanak, Tunisia, Senegal, Afghanistan, Ivory Coast, Cambodia and so on. They haunt the woods, for those who care to listen. Some have been here for a century, others for just a few weeks. An Egyptian, born in 1984, died on 26 May 2023 in detention. His name has not been revealed. He complained about chest pains in the night, fell asleep and never woke up.[1] The man lost his life a short walk away from the Garden for Tropical Agronomy, in the Centre of Administrative Retention, a form of administrative detention for asylum seekers and immigrants waiting for their status to be checked, or waiting for their deportation.

The centre, located in the Gravelle redoubt, a fort built at the same time as the Thiers Wall, shares its facility with a police school. It is hidden in the wood, and I struggle to find it. With its front gate at

Ruins of the Morrocan Pavilion in the Garden
for Tropical Agronomy, in 2023.

Statue of Eugène Napoléon Étienne overgrown by plants
and trees, Garden of Tropical Agronomy, in 2023.

one's back, where the words *Liberté, Égalité, Fraternité* are written on a red, white and blue banner, one can see the posh Vincennes racetrack. The building mixes nineteenth-century military architecture with the typical devices of modern prisons: high walls, barbed wires, cameras. I had planned to take a picture but faced with a dozen policemen and the hostility of the site, I chicken out.

Created in January 1959, the centre had then a similar role, but its name did not have the veneer of today's migration policy jargon: it was the *Centre de triage de Vincennes*, the centre for 'sorting out' immigrants.[2] Created by the prefect of police of Paris Maurice Papon, it was specifically aimed to detain Algerians living in France, arrested or rounded up by the police, to check their identity and visa status. As in 2023, the detainees denounced overcrowding, insults, racist slurs and acts of violence – head struck against the wall (2023), feet hit with a bullwhip (1960), general physical assaults (1960 and 2023), toes crushed with a truncheon (1960).

Papon, a former prefect in Constantine, Algeria, was one of the most powerful civil servants of the 1960s, decorated with the Legion of Honour in 1961 by de Gaulle in person. In 1998, he was convicted for complicity in crimes against humanity for his role in the deportation of Jews to Drancy and then to Auschwitz, while he was a high-ranking civil servant in Bordeaux during the war. Meanwhile, his role in the bloody repression against the Algerians and those that supported their independence in Paris, which I will touch on in this chapter, will be judged only by the trial of history.

The history of Paris space is hardwired into French colonialism. The vocabulary of urban planning in the twentieth century, the tools of city-making, the philosophy of control, the toponomy, the resources violently extracted from the colonies that built Paris – all form the colonial heritage of the capital city. And of course, there are the men and women that live in Paris today, those that lived here before: immigrant workers, political exiles, students, soldiers from colonised countries who came to fight in Europe to defend the 'motherland', the colons (French settlers) who came back after colonies achieved independence, the civil servants who made part of their careers in the colonies, the soldiers and the policemen.

People, ideas, prejudices, hatreds, memories, trauma, stigma and political and social projects travel back and forth across times and geographies to form the complex entanglement of Paris's identity today. In this chapter, I will touch upon only the surface of this multifaceted, convoluted and painful set of histories in their relation to Paris urban planning. Among them is a French spatial myth that has travelled the world over, just like the Eiffel Tower and Mona Lisa: the banlieue, the 'margins of the Empire' in the words of Louisa Yousfi, the author of *Rester barbare* (We will always be barbarians).[3] To get there, let us continue our journey where we started it, in the Bois de Vincennes.

In parallel to Haussmann's reorganisation of Paris, the Bois de Vincennes and Bois de Boulogne were donated to the city in the 1860s, to offer two 'green lungs' to Parisians. The Bois de Boulogne, exclusively dedicated to leisure, surrounded by posh suburban towns and neighbourhoods, is the *domaine réservé* of Paris's bourgeoisie and aristocracy. West of the city, the park is poorly connected to the city centre and working-class districts. The Bois de Vincennes, on the other hand, is surrounded by a more diverse fabric of suburban towns and Parisian districts – from the snobbish but charming Vincennes to more socially diverse Fontenay-Sous-Bois, headed by a Communist mayor since 1965. It is also closer to the city's blue-collar arrondissements (eleventh, twelfth, thirteenth, nineteenth, twentieth) – though, today, the working-class population has mostly been priced out of the city proper. But the Bois de Vincennes also has a darker, more complex history that remains in the shadows for most of its visitors. The *bois* was strongly connected to the army until its progressive and only partial demilitarisation starting in 1947. While many of the former buildings have been repurposed for leisure – for instance, the theatre of the Cartoucherie, a former cartridge factory – others are maintained as an infrastructure of state violence, such as the Gravelle redoubt that I have already mentioned.

The *bois*, which the army never completely abandoned, is actually about to regain a new stature in state security when the French secret services move their headquarters there in 2028, onto the site of a former military camp. But Vincennes also has a long-lasting relationship to race and colonialism, which started with the tropical plants and human zoos of Nogent-sur-Marne before hosting the acme of imperial France's cultural project: the Great Colonial Exhibition of 1931.

On 6 May 1931, the president of the Republic Gaston Doumergue officially opened the Paris Colonial Exhibition. A silent newsreel shows the president's motorcade escorted by Moroccan spahis on horseback, driving through the Bois de Vincennes that had been reimagined as a grandiose colonial fair. Spread over 110 hectares, the imposing exhibition offered its visitors pavilions representing the extent and might of the French colonial empire: Senegal, Ivory Coast, Mauritania, Algeria, Togo, Cameroon, Syria and Lebanon, Guadeloupe, Martinique, Madagascar, Morocco, Indochina and so on. The list was long. Reproductions of local architecture – including an impressive reconstruction of the temple complex of Angkor Wat (Cambodia), the focal point of the exhibition – were displayed alongside modernist buildings mixed with reinterpretations of vernacular design.

The reconstruction of the temple of Ankor Wat at
the Colonial Exhibition of Vincennes.

Pavilions and shops for private companies (Nestlé, Banania, Menier Chocolate, the French publisher Hachette), for churches (Catholic and Protestant) and for foreign countries were also erected. France had invited all colonial powers, but only a handful accepted the invitation – Italy (Libya, Somalia), Denmark (Greenland), Belgium (Congo), the United States of America (Alaska), the Netherlands (Malaysia) and Portugal (Angola, Mozambique, Macao, among others). The British Empire, for instance, had politely declined, arguing they were too busy finalising the Commonwealth of Nations, founded with the Statute of Westminster in December of the same year.

This celebration of the 'greater France', a slogan coined in 1903, also came at a time when France's colonial empire had started to teeter, with anticolonial movements gaining momentum both in the colonised territories and in France – I will come back to that in a moment. Yet on the surface, the exhibition was a total success, with an estimated 8 million visitors. The political and cultural project it supported was meant to reaffirm the power of France, enticing a new generation of entrepreneurs to move to the colonies, while indoctrinating French youth to consider the resources, landscapes, colours, music, food, architecture and peoples they saw in Vincennes as theirs.

Six kilometres long, three and a half kilometres wide and endowed with its own railway, the exhibition had mobilised hundreds of thousands of workers for its construction, including many artists, architects and artisans from across the colonies. The

Bird-eye-view of the Paris Colonial Exhibition
of 1931 in the Bois de Vincennes.

line 8 of the *métro* had even been extended up to a new station called
Porte Dorée, a 'golden gate' to access a colonial world of wonders —
which said absolutely nothing of the extreme violence colonialism
entailed, obviously.

The creation of this temporary colonial 'wonderland', which had
been in the making for decades, was the grand success of one man
whose figure embodied colonialism for the French public and abroad.
In the silent news clip I described earlier, he sits by the president in
the parading car, easily recognisable with his brush cut, curly mous-
tache and grand military uniform: Hubert Lyautey, Marshal of France.

Like most officers of his generation, Lyautey spent his career
fighting France's colonial wars to extend the empire. Following in
the steps of his mentor Joseph Gallieni, Lyautey led campaigns of
'pacification' — that terrible colonial euphemism — in Algeria,
Indochina and Madagascar, which mixed crushing local resistance
with developing new infrastructure to organise space, extract
resources and subjugate the population. Lyautey's legacy, his *grande
oeuvre*, was the 'conquest' of Morocco (1907–12), which became a
French protectorate from 1912 until 1956, with Lyautey as its first
resident general until 1925.

The heritage of Lyautey in France and Morocco is both equivocal
and more complex than that of many of the French colonialists of the
nineteenth and twentieth centuries. I will leave these touchy debates
to specialised historians, but his role in the urban planning of
Moroccan cities and its connection to Paris's is important to mention.
Inspired by British colonialism, Lyautey relied on existing political
structures in place in Morocco — while favouring the emergence of
leaders that might serve France's interest — instead of destroying and
imposing a reorganisation of the social system of the country as the

French did in other colonies. He developed a similar approach to urban planning, a domain he was fascinated by.

In the summary of the Congress on Colonial Urban Planning that took place at the colonial exhibition in October 1931, Lyautey writes in the foreword:

> During my long colonial career, I have been passionate about two issues: Indigenous Policy and Urbanism. Indigenous Policy is the foundation of our colonial life, of our progression, of pacification, of populations' support, of our union with them always growing stronger, of all that makes our colonial endeavour great and noble, constructive and not destructive, as I have so often said. Urbanism . . . is of the same family as the Indigenous Policy. It brings the enjoyment of life, comfort, charm and beauty.[4]

Lyautey was close to the Musée Social and was one of the personalities that supported the creation of the French Society for Urban Planners in 1911. He associated colonialism with the building of new cities such as this, as he wrote in 1897, 'little town of Ankazobé[, Madagascar], for which I had myself drawn the map in the sand and now I was watching it grow, house by house, avenue after avenue, tree after tree, with a paternal feeling'.[5] In December 1913, advised by the president of the Musée Social Georges Risler, Lyautey hired the architect Henri Prost to work on the urban planning of Moroccan cities.

In 1902, Prost had won the Grand Prix of Rome, France's most prestigious architectural award, and spent three years at Villa Medici in Italy studying the design of Byzantine cities before truly pivoting to city planning when he won the international competition for the city masterplan of Anvers, Belgium, in 1910. Prost later gave his name to an important strategic planning document for the redevelopment of the Paris region, completed in 1934 but never implemented.

In Morocco, joined by leading French architects and planners such as Albert Laprade, Prost was commissioned to design new cities abiding by the principles of modern urbanism while preserving the architectural and cultural heritage of the existing urban fabric.

This was the spatial manifestation of Lyautey's 'indigenous policy', where two separated 'urban orders' limited the mixing of populations: 'Europeans' in the new towns and 'Muslims' in the medinas. On the one hand, Lyautey's policy respected the old towns and preserved their architectural heritage, which he admired; on the other, it created a form of apartheid that separated populations based on race, religion and class.[6] In Rabat, Casablanca, Fez, Marrakech, 'European cities' or 'new towns', excrescences of the old 'indigenous' towns, were designed – often structured around the French military camps that could protect the colons in case of rebellion. The urban planning philosophy tapped into a pseudo impossibility for the colons and the Moroccans to live together in the same district: 'Muslim life cannot make do with living next to the Europeans, and our lifestyle cannot adapt to Muslims' rules', writes Prost in 1932 while also denouncing the 'physiological destitution and uncleanliness [of the natives] that are important factors in the spread of diseases'.[7]

We recognise here the discourse and lexical field that urban planners also used in France to describe ragpickers' dwellings and the Zone, working-class districts, Jewish neighbourhoods and so on. The two cities, European and indigenous, needed to be clearly separated in space, to avoid the two 'orders' mingling. In Fez, Prost enacted a zone *non-ædificandi* between the new and old towns, an area where construction was forbidden, to mark the separation between the two cities – just like the Zone outside Paris. The separation was reaffirmed in the introduction to the published summary of the Congress on Colonial Urban Planning of 1931 that I already cited: 'It is necessary

– also out of concern for the whites' health – *never to mingle in a city the indigenous and European populations.* It is a truth that Marshal Lyautey has made law. We cannot recommend enough to enforce it.'[8]

The italics, which are in the original text, stress the importance of this rule. Though this 'truth' created a clash with urban planners from other colonial countries, who opposed it during the congress that they also attended. And so, in the final list of commands that was voted by the assembly and presented by Henri Prost, the third 'wish' expressed that

> satellite towns separated by screens of greenery should be designed, but any measures that would prevent the contact and collaboration of races should be avoided.[9]

We find here an oxymoronic compromise reached by the congress: enforcing a spatial segregation, yes, but one that should not prevent contact between social and racial groups. We also encounter again a device that is now familiar to us, a green belt, used not as space for leisure but as a *screen*. We could discuss the choice of words here – a screen, *écran* in French, is not a hard border but something that masks or filters, something through which an illusion is broadcasted. Yet the idea of separation, of hiding racial and religious communities from one another, was reaffirmed as one of the founding principles of colonial urbanism's guidelines.

In 1927, two years after leaving Morocco, Marshal Lyautey was appointed chief curator of the Paris Colonial Exhibition. Several locations were envisioned, including the Bois de Boulogne in the west, and the Champs de Mars by the Eiffel Tower. But the city and the state eventually agreed on the Bois de Vincennes. An odd choice for many, as it was a neighbourhood where neither French elites nor tourists frequented. But Lyautey supported the decision (which was made before his appointment). In a speech in 1928 he declared:

> We are going to settle in the centre of underprivileged neighbourhoods, where lives a population that is not much used to seeing a large number of people coming to them . . . It is interesting, it is very interesting to go and plant our colonial seeds in this working-class world where nine-tenths of the population is only separated from us because of some incomprehension . . . I am excited to meet this population and to have a chat with them. I am convinced the Exhibition can be a great factor of social peace in this part of Paris.[10]

The parallels between colonial urbanism and the way Lyautey refers to the working-class population of Paris are transparent. The same way French urban planners offered 'civilisation' to colonised peoples by building new towns – mainly reserved for European settlers – they would do so in Vincennes as well, by planting the 'seeds of colonialism' to defeat ignorance, poverty, lack of hygiene and – ultimately – communism, compared to a disease that thrived on misery.

As we have seen in the chapter on the Red Belt, Delouvrier would speak of communism in the banlieue more or less in the same terms, thirty years later. On the edges of Paris, right outside the Zone *non-ædificandi*, a new town would be created – an excrescence of working-class Paris. A temporary city, a colonial wonderland to 'pacify' the eastern districts and the nearby banlieue. This recalls the analysis of the political scientist Françoise Vergès: 'What they learned in the colonies, they applied to all rebels. Because the bayonets were also used to crush working-class revolts in France and the glorified generals represented as statues never hesitated to fulfil their desires against working classes once back in France.'[11]

In a powerful, concise book on colonialism in Paris's public space, Vergès, a leading antiracist and decolonial intellectual, proposes an analysis of present-day Porte Dorée, which she calls a 'colonial triangle' – its three corners being the golden statue of France represented as Athena and originally titled *France Bringing Peace and Prosperity to the Colonies*; a monument to the colonialist Jean-Baptiste Marchand; and the Palais de la Porte Dorée, an overwhelming Art Deco building erected for the colonial exhibition that still stands today.

Indeed, not all architectural traces of the Paris Colonial Exhibition have disappeared. The pavilions for Togo and Cameroon are still standing in the Bois de Vincennes, transformed into a Buddhist centre and temple renamed the Pagoda of Vincennes – which hosts the largest Buddha of Europe. Two others were moved: the Catholic church was transferred to Épinay, a suburban town in Seine-Saint-Denis, in a contribution to the evangelisation of the red suburbs of Paris; the American pavilion, an exact replica of Mount Vernon – the master's house of George Washington's plantation, where hundreds of slaves worked for him – was bought by a private investor and transferred to the bourgeois city of Vaucresson, west of Paris. The house goes regularly on sale – if you have a few million to spare.

But the most imposing building still standing from the 1931 exhibition is the Palais de la Porte Dorée, which today houses France's Museum of the History of Immigration and . . . a tropical aquarium. The building had several names that reflect France's difficult and evolving relationship to colonialism – and the world: 'Museum of the Colonies' (1931), 'Museum of the Colonies and Exterior France' (1932), 'Museum of Overseas France' (1935), 'Museum of African and Oceanian Arts' (1960) and 'National Museum for Arts from

Africa and Oceania' (from 1990 until its closure in 2003). This is when most of its art collections were transferred to the Musée du Quai Branly that opened in 2006, while a controversial curatorial project dedicated to the history of immigration in France was created in the former colonial museum in 2007.

From the outset, the building was intended to remain the only permanent construction of the colonial exhibition. Designed by Albert Laprade – who worked with Prost in Morocco and would also design Lyautey's tomb in Les Invalides several decades later – it is an Art Deco building with a touch of Stripped Classicism, together with evocations of the arts and artisanship of the colonies. Lyautey preferred to hire Le Corbusier, but eventually reluctantly accepted Laprade's design in 1928 as time was running out to develop yet another project for the opening.[12] The building was adorned with a ninety-metre-long, thirteen-metre-high bas-relief that covers the entire facade, and remains in place today. It depicts a dominating allegory of France, surrounded by representations of the French colonies and the products they cultivated as well as the planes and boats that symbolise the technological domination of France over peoples depicted as primitive.

For Vergès, this immense frieze that represents the colonial process of extraction – which, she adds, continues to this day – is the fabrication of an 'illusion': that of the 'successful pacification of an empire busy working' at a time when anticolonial voices grew stronger, and started to unite across peoples, countries and empires. In France, the Communist Party and artists of the surrealist movement denounced the exhibition: 'This apotheosis is that of crime', wrote *L'Humanité*, while on opening day in May 1931, Paul Éluard, André Breton, Tristan Tzara, Louis Aragon and others were in Vincennes distributing leaflets that discouraged visitors from entering and a counterexhibition, 'The Truth About the Colonies', was shown in central Paris.

In Morocco, Algeria, Indochina and Sub-Saharan African countries, a range of anti-imperialist demonstrations had taken place in the two decades that preceded the exhibition: from military uprisings and localised rebellions to the creation of anticolonial newspapers, publication of books and pamphlets and singing of songs and poetry – the resistance was growing ever more vocal.

The first Pan-African Congress was held in Paris in 1919, followed by other editions in Lisbon, Brussels, London and New York City in 1921, 1923 and 1927. In 1927, the influential League for the Defense of the Negro Race was created by, among others, the politician and unionist Tiemoko Garan Kouyaté, born in French Sudan (present-day Mali), and the Senegalese political activist Lamine Senghor. In reaction to the Paris Colonial Exhibition, a diverse opposition coalesced – diverse in the forms, voices and countries of origin of its main actors – striving to create an intercolonial solidarity against the imperial powers and the message of the exhibit in Vincennes.

The golden statue of France as Athena stands today at the centre of Porte Dorée, a few metres from the steps of the colonial museum where it was originally placed.

The goddess of wisdom, strategy and war that was meant to bring peace and prosperity to the French colonial empire ironically watches over a tiny garden dedicated in 1987 to the veterans of the Indochina War – the French defeat that acted as a beacon of hope across the colonies.

On 7 May 1954, 9,000 kilometres away from Porte Dorée, the last French positions were overtaken by the Việt Minh forces of General Võ Nguyên Giáp in the Battle of Điện Biên Phủ, present-day Vietnam. The Communist and nationalist political organisation

Statue of France as Athena in present-day Square of Indochina veterans.

created in May 1941 to free Vietnam from French colonisation had
defeated the great European power, which would leave the newly
independent country a few months after the blaring defeat. The fall
of Điện Biên Phủ had an astounding echo across the colonies – and
in France. The French, despite their equipment, infrastructure, military training and available funds, could be beaten. Vietnam in 1954
became the first of what Frantz Fanon has called a 'guide territory', a
term he coined in reference to Algeria's fight for independence:

> Between colonised peoples there seems to be some kind of illuminating and
> sacred communication which means that each freed territory is, for a time,
> promoted to being a 'guide territory'. The independence of a new terri-
> tory, the liberation of new peoples are felt by other oppressed countries as
> an invitation, an encouragement, and a promise. Each setback in the colo-
> nial domination in America and Asia reinforces the national will of African
> peoples. It is in the national struggle against the oppressor that colonised
> peoples have discovered, concretely, the solidarity across the colonialist
> block and the necessary interdependency of liberation movements.[13]

So wrote the Afro-Caribbean psychiatrist and intellectual in the pages
of Algerian National Liberation Front's (FLN) guerrilla information
bulletin *El Moudjahid* in 1958. The movement for freedom had inexorably started: independence was obtained by Lebanon and Syria in
1946, Vietnam in 1954, Morocco and Tunisia in 1956, Guinea in 1958,
Togo, Cameroon, Madagascar, Ivory Coast and all Sub-Saharan
colonies in 1960. But there was one country whose independence the
French would not accept.

Not considered a colonised country but a region integral to France,
extending 'from Dunkirk to Tamanrasset', as de Gaulle proclaimed
in 1958, that country was Algeria. The war for independence in

Algeria had direct repercussions in mainland France and on the urbanism of Paris.

The nineteenth century had been dominated by migrations of people from different regions of France – Brittany, Savoie, Auvergne – who formed networks based on counties of origin and language (Bretons often did not speak French), occupying certain districts of Paris and 'specialising' in specific trades (Bretons became maids, Auvergnats sold wine and coal and so on). The second half of the nineteenth and first half of the twentieth centuries saw an increase in international migration – Italians, Poles, Belgians, Swiss, Russians and, to a lesser extent, Northern Africans and Spanish, who fled dire economic or hostile political situations in their home countries.

After World War II, the situation was starkly different. Close to 600,000 French individuals had died in the global conflict, the majority of whom were civilians, and millions were left homeless and hundreds of thousands of buildings had been permanently damaged or destroyed entirely. France, which was about to enter a period of prosperity, economic growth and self-confidence, which economists later called the Thirty Glorious Years, first needed manpower to rebuild, and international immigration was seen as the key.

Three main groups of immigrants moved to France from the 1940s until the early 1980s: Spanish, Portuguese and Northern Africans (mostly Algerians, then Moroccans and Tunisians). Migrants from Spain pushed out during the 1930s by the fascist dictator Francisco Franco's persecutions were joined by a new wave of Spanish immigrants fleeing misery and a reactionary, authoritarian society. Meanwhile, the Portuguese moved to France illegally to escape poverty and avoid serving four years in the army during the years of António de Oliveira Salazar's dictatorship, which had initiated an offensive against liberation movements in the Portuguese colonies.

Northern Africans, and specifically Algerians, who moved to France represented a very different case. While the number of immigrants from Morocco and Tunisia was initially modest, before picking up in the late 1980s, the number of Algerians moving to France increased quickly after 1945 to reach 212,000 individuals in 1954 and more than 400,000 in 1962, when the country became independent.[14] Algerian immigration to France was different in comparison to other colonies, including other countries of the Maghreb, because Algeria was a *département* of France and Algerians were French nationals. Though they had the special status of 'French Muslim from Algeria' (FMA), theoretically, they were granted the same rights as any French citizen.

While some limits were implemented in 1956, Algerians could, for instance, travel freely between France and Algeria and work in France without certain restrictions, such as work visas, that immigrants from other colonies had to deal with. Many Algerians, especially in rural communities, lived in extreme poverty, with generalised malnutrition and localised episodes of famine. France needed an extra workforce and had higher salaries to offer, leading Algerian men to migrate to France – the majority to Paris – to work in factories and on construction sites, leaving their families in Algeria, whom they supported by sending money back home.

For both the immigrants and the French authorities, this situation was meant to be temporary. There was no desire for immigrants to stay in France, and neither the French public nor the successive governments would consider having them remain in the country and become an integral part of French society.

Northern Africans that arrived in France had to endure mainstream xenophobia, fuelled by a long history of racism and colonialism that had depicted brown and black individuals from the colonies as 'subhuman' and 'savage'. They also had limited financial resources upon arriving, and those from the working classes experienced the shock of an entirely new lifestyle, set of habits and weather. These men had access to two main types of accommodation: hostels for Algerian workers and, more commonly, furnished rooms in private hotels. Social housing and privately rented flats were out of reach.

Built to face the increasing number of workers, hostels were supervised by the Ministry of the Interior, often in partnership with the private companies that hired Algerians. While the official reasons to build these hostels were to fight discrimination against Algerians in France and save them from predatory landlords, the underlying strategy was to maximise the force that could be extracted from their bodies by offering decent accommodation while enforcing social and police control. As historian Samia Henni has shown in her book *Architecture of Counterrevolution: The French Army in Northern Algeria*, these hostels constituted an extension of 'pacification' strategies in mainland France.[15] Overseen by 'managers' that were often former soldiers and policemen in the colonies, the hostels provided accommodation in dorms of six to twenty beds located in buildings erected in a hurry at the expense of construction standards.

If living conditions were initially slightly less catastrophic than in private hotels, the state of these buildings decayed rapidly – because of their initial design, bad construction and lack of maintenance. Hostels specifically built for Algerian workers, later opened to people of other nationalities, were a typical example of the amalgamation of social service and policing that characterised the situation of Algerian immigrants up until 1962.

The quick-paced decay of these buildings was blamed on the origins, not to say the race and religion, of those that inhabited them instead of poor construction: an association between dirt, animality, backwardness and ethno-racial identity. This deteriorating situation reached its apex – at least in public opinion – in January 1970 when five immigrant workers, four Senegalese and one Mauritanian, living in a hostel in Aubervilliers, died during the night on New Year's Eve, intoxicated by a makeshift heating solution they had set up to cope with poor insulation and below-zero temperatures. 'According to the early findings of the inquiry, it seems the tenants of the "French-African Solidarity Hostel" could not pay extra for heating', writes *Le Monde*, underlining the bitter irony of the accommodation's title, before giving the names of the dead and injured.[16]

Hostels were far from offering enough rooms to accommodate the constantly growing number of immigrants that, most commonly, ended up finding lodging in furnished hotels. No matter one's origin, furnished hotels had always been the traditional landing points for immigrants in Paris (and remain so to this day). They offered austere but practical, cheap and flexible modes of occupation (paying per night or weekly). Northern Africans often found rooms in hotels they had been recommended to, owned by someone from the same village, or where a family member or a friend already lived. The Franco-Algerian academic Abdelmalek Sayad, a foremost sociologist of immigration active from the 1960s until his death in 1998, whose study on Algerians in Nanterre I have relied on extensively in this chapter, writes about a hotel on 69 Rue Paul Morin, where

we find in 1953, out of 80 tenants, 29 individuals that come from the same village as the owner, a great number that comes from the same *douar* [an administrative entity slightly bigger than a village in colonial Algeria], and so, except a dozen residents (2 Moroccans, 5 people from Oran [in Algeria]

and 3 others from the regions of M'Sila and Biskra [in Algeria]), all tenants
came from the county of Tizi-Ouzou [in Algeria].[17]

Living conditions, which were already precarious and, to say the
least, did not offer much comfort, decayed even quicker as rooms
became overcrowded. In the early 1950s, demand for housing
exceeded the supply on offer, which had already been stretched far to
accommodate immigrants and take their cash – for instance, by rent-
ing out the same bed to several workers working on night and day
shifts, or transforming damp cellars and garden sheds into dorms.

> The overcrowding of hotels and the resulting extreme promiscuity, the
> deterioration of the buildings, the very bad hygiene conditions, the
> complete lack of maintenance including for the toilets that were simply
> removed in many cases, all this had turned these furnished hotels for North
> Africans into genuine slums . . . This occupation of a disintegrating space
> appears as a transition, a preparation to life in the *bidonville*. One already
> lived in furnished hotels turned into *bidonville*.[18]

Bidonville, literally 'tin-city', is the French translation of 'slum' or
'shanty town'. Like the word 'slum', *bidonville* encapsulates a moral
judgement and social reform project: a confusion so pervasive in the
global history of urban planning, where a dominant group sets a
norm, then moves on to destroy what does not fit the norm. But
bidonville has a racial and colonial twist added to it. The origins of the
word are murky but probably come back to 1930s Tunisia or Morocco.
It is said that there was a 'monstrous town' on the outskirts of
Casablanca in the 1930s built by migrant workers from corrugated
iron, old tin and cardboard.[19] The original nickname, Gadoueville
(meaning Mud City), did not do well, and someone – a journalist? a

planner? a local? – came up with Bidonville, which caught on beyond all expectation.

From a specific toponymy, the word became a common name that French planners had picked up in the colonies and brought back to mainland France to describe the shanty towns in the banlieue of Paris, built by the same immigrant workers that had joined France from Northern Africa. There was nothing specific, nor anything new about postwar *bidonvilles* – except the nationalities of their inhabitants. The history of cities is also that of informal makeshift housing made of salvaged materials, and there are arguably more shared features between the informal housing settlements built across time and space than with the architecture of bricks and mortar savant books focus on.

The Zone of Paris was in French urban planning culture the archetypal slum before the invention of the word *bidonville*. While not all *bidonvilles* were inhabited by Northern Africans – there were Spanish, Portuguese and more rarely Italian *bidonvilles* in Paris – the term was most immediately associated with immigrants from Tunisia, Morocco and Algeria. And from the 1950s until its dismantlement in the 1970s, the largest and most iconic *bidonville* was in the city of Nanterre, a few kilometres west of Paris.

At the time, Nanterre was a working-class town that was slowly moving out of the semi-rurality typical of a Paris suburb in the middle of the twentieth century – offering a mix of detached houses built in the previous century when the town was surrounded by countryside, low-density industrial plants, brownfields, railroad infrastructure and empty land earmarked for some distant development. There, in the middle of an abandoned military facility, appeared one makeshift house, then two, three, ten, fifty, a hundred. The first houses of the *bidonville* were connected to the hotels, which sought to provide more accommodations to prospective tenants. They bought or rented empty pieces of land close to their establishments and had one or two barracks built.

Others followed suit, building new makeshift houses nearby and bringing their families. Indeed, a major change had taken place in Algerian immigration trends: starting in the mid-1950s, instead of single men seeking work, immigrants were more often whole families – husbands, wives and children – fleeing Algeria, which had become a war zone. The war for independence had spilled over, it would be fought on French soil too, and Nanterre became the terrain for a dirty, stealthy, bloody fight.

The families that had stayed behind while the men worked in France had faced the horrors of a war that reached new levels of violence daily, targeting fighters and civilians as the inevitable outcome of an independent Algeria grew more certain. Harassment, torture, murders, rapes, destruction of crops, tearing down of homes, bombing of entire areas with napalm, areas declared 'forbidden' and population transferred to 'displacement camps' – all these actions were carried out by the French Army. Fetched by their husbands and fathers or sent to them without notice by their families and friends to escape the worst, Algerian wives and children traveled to Marseille by boat and to Paris by plane, their heads filled with the atrocities they had experienced.

Yasmîna, the wife of Tâhar ... her face furrowed with grief, had just arrived in the patched-up shack with her six-year old child ... Before coming, Yasmîna had dug the earth, in secret, with the help of her neighbours, to lay down five bodies, all family members, killed overnight. Her nineteen-year-old son, massacred in front of her by the French Army. Three uncles shot dead. And her dad killed in front of her: a soldier shot him in the head. She watched as, detached from its socket, his eye fell into her father's hand and the bullet exited on the other side of the skull. And before that, Yasmîna had lost three children because there were no doctors. Yasmîna describes her life in Algeria. 'The soldiers of France shot at anything that moved.' Houses burned down. Cannons aiming at villages. Men hanged. Or thrown into ravines. Many of the women, of the teenagers in the [*bidonville*] have lived through these horrors.[20]

Fâtiha, thirteen years old:

Their *douar* was only inhabited by women, kids and elderly. She can't help seeing again and again the vision of this Algerian woman burned alive by the army in the middle of the village. 'Like Joan of Arc', she tells me. She sees again the burn marks of cigarettes on women's bosoms. 'They cover men with honey, I saw it. All their bodies, so that the wasps, the fleas come and they leave them like that in the scorching sun.' She remembers, 'They force women to drink soapy water and then the French soldiers jumped on their stomachs. The foam comes out from everywhere, from the anus, from the mouth, and the soldiers they laugh, they laugh . . .' Big tears run down from her dark, piercing eyes, like those of a tiger.[21]

Those testimonies, among a dozen others, were recorded by Monique Hervo in her diary. Hervo was a fascinating, courageous character, whose notes, photographs and interviews are invaluable material that for decades documented the life of Algerians in the *bidonville* of Nanterre. She had trained to become a stained-glass artisan, to rebuild the churches of France destroyed by the war, but she discovered the *bidonville* of Nanterre in 1959 when working for an NGO, and eventually lived there until 1971. Her diary offers an uncompromising account of the life there and the daily harassment of Algerians in France.

The men, these husbands and fathers who toiled in France for their families back in Algeria, had not built cosy homes for themselves. Their presence was meant to be temporary, and all money that could be spared was sent back home. With no warning – sometimes a telegram was sent by a relative bluntly announcing that his family was on their way, with the time of their plane's landing in Orly – the men had to find accommodation quickly in a housing landscape where family flats with private landlords and social housing were mostly out of reach – because of racism, cost and the criteria of eligibility. The *bidonville* would be their cursed liberation.

Abdelmalek Sayad describes the shanty towns of Paris. The long journey to fetch drinking water in the single access point outside the settlement, the torrents that ran down the alleys when it rained too much, threatening to take away the shacks, the absence of mains drainage and, of course, no pavement or macadam. And the mud everywhere. The mud on the clothes that singled you out as belonging to the *bidonville*, a mark of 'infra-humanity' that brought mockery from the white coworkers and reproaches by the boss, and that forced you to walk two hours across Paris instead of taking the risk of being denied boarding by the bus driver.[22]

Fire was another great fear. In shacks with makeshift roofs covered with tar, where the light, heating and cooking relied on candles and open fire, or more rarely on hacked electricity, the risk of fire breaking out was constant. The proximity of the shacks meant a fire could spread quickly across the *bidonville*. One of Sayad's interviewees explains:

We're always wary of fire. You need to watch out and shout, raise the alarm as soon as you see smoke. You can't wait. You sacrifice all the water

you have gathered and we go for it together . . . until the fire brigade
arrives. It takes time, we don't have the telephone and fire lorries struggle
to reach us.[23]

And then there were the rats:

The rats were everywhere, in the shacks, outside the shacks, on the surface
and below ground. They speak about them with a language almost military: they are legions, they are an uncountable army, they invade, they
assault, they do not respect anything. Nothing resists them. They eat us
away, they destroy us, they take our food away. We cannot hide anything
from them, we cannot escape them. They are stronger than us . . . We are
afraid for our babies, they can eat them alive.[24]

There are countless stories in Hervo's diary of adults, children and
babies being bitten by rats and then rushed to hospitals. Rats prolifer-
ated in the *bidonville*. There were barely any boundaries between the
inside and the outside of shacks, latrines were holes dug in the ground
by the house and filled up with soil once full, waste – food and other
types – was disposed of as far as possible from home in open-air land-
fills. To clear the landfill, the pile of waste was regularly set on fire.
The municipalities did not include the *bidonville* in the refuse collection, because officially, it did not exist.

But the ultimate fear, the one above all else, was the fear of men.
The fear of the police, the fear of the civil servants, the fear of the
French State. The *bidonville* is just fear.

We are always afraid, and our wives, and our children are always afraid.
Afraid of everything. Of the skies, of the earth, of the rain, of the sun, of
the fire. And especially afraid of men: gendarmes, CRS, police, all civil

servants: afraid of ourselves. How can you not be afraid when you know you are not allowed to live here, *that you do not exist* . . . *We* have reasons to be afraid, we know why. Everything and everyone is against us so we are always afraid. But I think they too are afraid of us. We did not do anything, we didn't bite them, we didn't attack them. Quite the opposite, we just ask not to be noticed, to be transparent, to be silent. But they are afraid of us. And we always hate what we're afraid of . . .[25]

In her diary, Hervo narrates the daily harassment from the police and the administration that only grew stronger as the war in Algeria intensified. It was a constant aggression against the French Muslims, to humiliate, to fight any resistance, to kill and destroy. The *bidonville* was a territory targeted by the police, by the Harkis – Algerians who fought alongside the French to keep Algeria a colony – and also a battleground for the two movements for Algeria's independence, MNA and FLN, that fought against each other for the control of Algerian communities in France.

With 1.5 million Frenchmen sent to fight the Algerian resistance, with attacks on French territory by the FLN, the OAS (a movement in favour of French Algeria that carried out a series of terrorist attacks, including two assassination attempts of de Gaulle), the tension was at its peak in Paris. Algerians in the *bidonvilles* were the main targets of the repression; they were, for many, the enemy within. Harassment passed through the civil servants: overnight they decided that postal addresses in the *bidonville* would not be recognised as legitimate, which meant the inhabitants could not renew their precious identity cards and visas.

City planners and policemen arrived in the camps with sledgehammers and, with no apparent logic and no prior notice, destroyed shacks and threatened to come back for the others. Arbitrariness was the norm, and humiliation the ultimate goal: a man was forbidden to dig a new hole for the family latrine or to build a light shack to surround the hole – forcing him and his family to urinate and defecate without privacy. Men, women and children were considered animals, were pushed to see themselves as animals – and were hunted down as such.

[February 1960] Around the *bidonville* of Bels-Ébats, where Algerian children play, I find several traps for wolves that have been set up there by evil hands. I inquire and find out that the French landlords of this place have had them placed here! Three kilometres away from the Champs-Élysées as the crow flies, what kind of prey did the G., an extremely wealthy family living in the poshest districts of Paris, expect to catch?[26]

Police controls were constant:

Police patrol in the flooded streets . . . At night, German shepherds look for arms cache. The glare of the searchlight intermittently lights up the corrugated iron roofs that have been weighted with stones to protect them from the wind gusts. A stone's throw away, the French, indifferent, live in peace.[27]

The police came up with any reason they could to arrest, beat up, torture or kill Algerians of the *bidonville*.

[26 January 1961] New raid of the police. A group of children run through the *bidonville* . . . 'The police, here comes the police', they shout out of breath. They lay low by some wall in a courtyard and Azdin calls to his friends: 'They're here, quick let's hide!' Hafid comes through. He shouts, 'The police, they're breaking down everything', warning as he goes the women busy doing the laundry . . . Further down, [men] with their hands on their heads, still, are lined up, their feet in the mud. With bludgeons, police are hitting them. For many months, this type of commando has operated.[28]

Arrested for driving too slowly, for presenting a damaged ID card (which had been torn up by policemen the day before), for looking suspicious – the Algerians were sent to local police station or to the detention centre of Vincennes where their identities, and their immigration statuses, were checked. Instead of the couple of hours required, they could be held for days in Vincennes, humiliated, beat up, tortured:

[17 May 1961] Abd al-Krim [was] arrested and sent to the identification centre of Vincennes. There policemen force him to remove his shoes and beat him up on his toes. His toes are crushed. Sent to hospital. Cannot go back to work. Already last year, he was tortured.[29]

[10 June 1961] Taking his daughter, who is on her way to a sanatorium, to Gare de Lyon, Mouahamad . . . was picked up by the police. They took him to Vincennes. He stayed there for several days and was beaten with a bullwhip.[30]

Hervo recounts another episode she experienced herself: a police van stopped and opened its door, and policemen pointed their machine guns at them. Abbâs, nicknamed the Good Man, whispered to her: 'Above all, do not move. It's like in Algeria, if you run they'll shoot you down.'[31] She also explains the constant threat of the Seine:

Mouhammad has disappeared. Is he in the camp in Vincennes? Lucky for him, to go to work, he does not have to walk on the bridge of Neuilly. There, policemen pick up and beat Algerians, then throw them out in the Seine river . . . I still hear them, threatening people of the Seine.

Then on 2 October 1961:

On this day, with great horror, the thousands of people living in the [*bidonville*] have learned from a respectable source (a highly placed civil servant with the police office) and this was confirmed by social workers in the camp, that recently the police have drowned twenty-five Algerians in the Seine. Consternation. The *bidonville* is in mourning. A great fear in all the shacks. Yet, despite the savage repression they face, each and every Algerian in the *bidonville* has never been so determined to fight for their country's independence.

In October 1961, the climate of violence in France was extreme. The roundups of Algerians and the assassinations by the Harkis and French police were carried out while the FLN murdered policemen in Paris. 'For each blow we receive, we will give them back ten,' announced Prefect of Police Maurice Papon in September during the burial of a policeman held in the courtyard of the police prefecture. The sentence was widely interpreted as a carte blanche to policemen. A few days later, on 5 October, a curfew on French Muslims from Algeria – and only them – was enacted: Algerians were told not to be out from 8:30 p.m. until 5:30 a.m., all cafés and bars owned or visited by French Muslims had to close at 7 p.m. and orders were given by the police to stop all cars driven by Algerians, arrest them and send the automobiles to the pound.

Then on the 17 October, something unbelievable happened. At around 6:30 p.m., all the inhabitants of the *bidonville* of Nanterre left their shacks. Men, women and children formed an immense cortege. The FLN had secretly organised a demonstration that would bring all Algerians to central Paris for a peaceful protest against the curfew. Meeting points had been set in République and Opéra, next to *métro* stations, while the Algerians of Nanterre – which had no metro line at the time – walked towards Paris to try to cross the Seine at Neuilly Bridge. At Opéra, most demonstrators were arrested by the police before they could exit the station and the cortege was aborted. At République, where many *métro* lines converged, the demonstration took shape and the crowd walked towards Opéra, taking the Grands Boulevards until they were violently stopped by the CRS in front of the Rex cinema. Meanwhile, in Nanterre, the crowd grew, joined by the Algerians from Puteaux, La Garenne, Bezons, Colombes. Monique Hervo writes:

People walk so closely one to another that I feel like it is a 'forest' walking down the avenue that leads to the Neuilly Bridge . . . Walking a quick step that seems unstoppable, shouting slogans sometimes, but mostly marching in an impressive silence, wave after wave, Algerians demonstrate sternly. They are thousands and thousands that progress stiffly with their resolution. They want the people of Paris to know that they will, whatever it costs, achieve their independence . . . This crowd descends on the entrance of the capital city. Startling vision . . .

Then shots are fired. The shootings break out between the roundabout of La Défense and the Neuilly bridge . . . We, the group of mothers and children, are then by the Rue Arago in Puteaux. The road is going down and so I can see clearly, down the avenue, a barrage of policemen in their dark uniforms. Cannons of rifles or machine guns are moving, aiming at the first ranks of the demonstration. Bullets are shot.[32]

In Nanterre, in Paris, the peaceful demonstration was countered with extreme violence by the police. Historians are still debating on the number of casualties: the estimates range from 38 to 200 Algerians murdered that night.

The French police had protected Paris from the French Muslims from Algeria, as they would have fought off an invading army or hordes of barbarians. They fatally shot unarmed protesters trying to cross the threshold of the city proper. City *proper* – I have always found that expression fascinating. A city for the proper people. It is also the 'proper' of 'property': one's own. For most Parisians, and their administration, the Algerians were not proper enough to be in Paris, they did not belong, they should not have access. In Hervo's diary, we find multiple references to Paris proper being a distant, dangerous city. A heavily policed urban environment, where the chances of being inspected and harassed were high. A very white city, where brown and black bodies stood out and were hunted down.

The Algerians won their independence a few months after the massacre of 17 October 1961, and the *bidonville* of Nanterre exploded in joyful cries and tears. It did not solve everything of course, nor did it stop immigration to France by Algerians, now foreign nationals. The *bidonville* of Nanterre, the furnished hotels and the hostels continued to flourish until the beginning of the 1970s. With the alleviation of the housing crisis, foreign nationals were finally granted easier access to other forms of tenancy, including those that had mushroomed right by the *bidonvilles*, a new urban typology of large-scale social housing: the *grands ensembles*.

In the immediate aftermath of the war, the housing situation in France was catastrophic. Two million housing units were destroyed in the conflict, and the home deficit inherited from the sluggish construction programme of the interwar period remained acute eight years after the Allied victory.[33] Nationally, in 1946, close to 2 million households were considered overcrowded and half a million were considered dilapidated. In Paris, 40 to 50 per cent of the population lived in over-crowded houses. Buildings in the city were old too, seventy-three years on average. In France, only 13 per cent of the housing stock had been built between 1919 and 1939, compared to 22 per cent in Germany, 30 per cent in England and 60 per cent in the Netherlands. In the capital city, buildings were often more comfortable than in other French towns – with 94 per cent of houses equipped with elec-tricity, gas and mains drainage – but only 18 per cent had a bathroom and toilets.[34]

Politics were slow to react to the urgency as they focused on economic growth instead. In 1952, while France built on average twenty housing units for 10,000 inhabitants per year, the United Kingdom built forty-seven and Germany ninety-nine.[35] Launched in 1946, the first five-year plan to rebuild and develop postwar France, named after its instigator, Jean Monnet, did not even mention hous-ing as its key priority. The situation was summed up by the demogra-pher and anthropologist Alfred Sauvy – who also coined the expres-sion 'Third World countries': 'The housing crisis [in France] is as much vigorously denounced as it is weakly fought against.' But a new dynamic was gaining momentum: a set of laws to fund and accelerate the path of construction passed in 1952 and 1953, and the terrible winter of 1953–4 would also be a wake-up call for politicians and civil society when Abbé Pierre, a Catholic priest and former MP who had founded the charity Emmaüs in 1949, made an appeal on the radio. That January 1954 had been particularly harsh: temperatures reached minus thirteen degrees Celsius in Paris overnight, and one could walk over the frozen Canal Saint-Martin. On the radio, Abbé Pierre made a passionate speech to the MPs and the government for urgent measures to address housing. A woman had frozen to death on Boulevard de Sébastopol in central Paris the night before, recounted Abbé Pierre; she still held her eviction notice in her hand.

The admonition was powerful, and people – at long last – reacted and took action. Civil society and the media brought the issue of housing to the forefront of what was not yet called the news cycle. Yet it would not be until the end of the 1950s that a mighty drive for the mass building of social housing would reach full throttle. One star model of urban planning–cum–architectural design became the go-to solution for the rapid construction of millions of flats across France: the *grands ensembles*, meaning 'great complexes' of buildings, though the expression could also be translated – ironically – as 'great together'.

Grands ensembles were social housing complexes the size of small towns built outside the city centre, sometimes on arable land in the peri-urban countryside. There, land was cheap, easy to secure and fast to acquire. A similar operation in the city centre would have taken years to realise, from consultation to eviction, destruction and then construction. All around Paris, in towns that were often more rural than urban, towers and rows of low-rise rectangular buildings – sometimes reaching half a kilometre in length – called *barres*, were quickly erected.[36] In Antony and Massy, Sarcelles, La Courneuve, le Blanc-Mesnil, Villiers-le-bel, Créteil and Garges-lès-Gonesses, social housing estates for tens of thousands of inhabitants were built over a few years.

In La Courneuve, the Cité des 4,000 – so named because it offered 4,000 homes – became one of the most iconic *grands ensembles* of the Paris region. The *nouvelle vague* director Jean-Luc Godard used this location to shoot his 1967 movie *Two or Three Things I Know About*

Her: the portrait of a housewife, an allegory for the Paris region, who occasionally prostitutes herself. The film opens with the construction site of the ring road and offers a critical association between capitalism, Paris modernist urban planning and the submission of Parisian bodies to this new, alienating space. In suburban industrial cities adjacent to Paris, the dilapidated town centres were also rebuilt with smaller-scale modernist *cités*, while on the former green belt of Paris, freed from its strict no-construction obligation, towers were erected right by the ring road already planned but not yet built, as we have seen with the Cité des Fougères.

At the outset, the improvement of living conditions in these estates was significant. The buildings came with bigger, brighter flats that were equipped with bathrooms, toilets and modern kitchens, and included amenities such as lifts and dedicated parking spaces. A whole city had also been imagined around them – with fast public transport, shops, public services, schools and markets. But the initial enthusiasm gradually waned: the amenities that had been promised did not materialise or were shut down because they were not economically viable; the buildings had been hastily designed and constructed and quickly deteriorated, while insulation from both noise and cold was deficient.

These *cités*, inspired by the CIAM and the modernist programmes of the 1930s, should have been designed as integral urban planning schemes, instead they were delivered as fast-paced construction projects – where housing was built first as a matter of urgency, with the rest following later. But it never did. The laurels went to the project that built the highest number of housing units in the shortest amount of time. Inhabitants of the Cité des 4,000, a programme built eight kilometres away from the city proper, ended up 'trapped' in their housing complex: with no public transport, no local amenities and buildings crumbling down on their heads, while the population could not hope to be rehoused anywhere else. The social housing of the Paris region soon acquired another stigma: immigration. In 1978, a young Sebastião Salgado shot pictures of life in La Courneuve's Cité des 4,000, at the request of a local Communist councillor friend of his. In 2014, the Brazilian photographer described his experience in La Courneuve to the *New York Times* as that of 'a migrant in a world of migrants'.[37] These pictures are a beautiful and touching portrait of La Courneuve – very different from the rest of Salgado's work in Africa and the Americas. They show a joyful, busy and diverse life in dire conditions, surrounded by shoddy architecture and deficient urban design. A few years back I reached out several times to Salgado's office for permission to reprint his pictures, but never received his approval. You will find a few browsing the internet, and the remainder is shared between the photographer's personal archives and the city's – which you are free to visit, with an appointment.

The immigrants that arrived in Paris and lived in *bidonvilles* often worked on the construction sites of the Paris region. They built the social housing blocks they were not allowed in. No law or decree openly prevented French Muslims from Algeria, or any other nationality, to access social housing. But the housing stock deficit was enormous and competition was rife. Access to social housing always includes a moral and social dimension: to be granted a house you need to be the perfect tenant, the *proper* tenant.

A decree published on 27 March 1954 illustrates this logic of exclusion. First, the decree defines that social housing should be limited to 'individuals without much wealth and workers living mostly from the wages they earn' – a very broad definition that potentially encompassed much of the French working and low-middle classes. In cities of 10,000 inhabitants or more, the applicants were marked according to a notation grid, whose criteria would be set out by the Ministry for Reconstruction and Housing, the Ministry for Public Health and the Ministry of the Interior. 'But', says the decree, 'social housing providers and public administrations can exclude from the final list any applicant that, after inquiry, would be unable to live in the flat peacefully as a reasonable man.'[38]

This paragraph enabled discrimination grounded in people's *perceived* capacity to live peacefully together based on countries of origin, ethno-racial identity and cultural traits. To regulate the origins of their tenants, institutions had established ethno-racial quotas. Their efforts to 'regulate' were made not only to exclude, but also to avoid creating 'ghettos' – concentrations of tenants of a single ethnic origin in one building, for instance. Unofficial occupancy rates – 10–15 per cent of foreigners – were quickly filled up. And of course, housing providers had room to pick which foreigners were 'good immigrants' – the Spanish, the Portuguese and the Italians being preferred to Northern Africans.

In the late 1960s, the idea of a *threshold of tolerance*, became widespread in public policy: to go over the threshold would make the cohabitation between the French and the immigrants unsustainable. The threshold concept came from a 1968 report that compared two *cités*, one (in Fontenay-le-Fleury, west of Versailles) where the immigrants were mostly Spanish and Italian, another (in Nanterre) where they were mostly Algerians. The report focused on the *visible presence* of Algerians, as opposed to the Italians and Spanish, whom French society considered to have a higher capacity to 'blend in'. Quotas, from a neocolonial device to mitigate against exclusion, became at the end of the 1960s a limit that should not be crossed, to avoid threatening the balance of French society.[39]

Postwar social housing was initially imagined for the lower-middle classes, not for the working classes and poorer elements of society. In the middle of the twentieth century, many blue-collar families where both parents worked could not access social housing – it was unaffordable. As the housing crisis dwindled, as the number of applicants decreased and, ultimately, as the middle classes' desire to become owner-occupiers instead of life-long renters increased, social housing providers had to take in the tenants they least wanted: immigrants and the poor.

In 1973, the year of the inauguration of the Boulevard Périphérique, a circular by the minister for infrastructure and housing forbade the construction of new large-scale housing complexes in the peripheries of large cities. The *grands ensembles* were loathed; they were a failure. They created, according to the minister, 'social segregation'. Just like the slums of nineteenth-century Paris, the *cités* of the banlieue represented the malady of twentieth-century urban planning, just a few years after their completion.

The disease even had a name – *sarcellitis*, a term coined after the suburban town of Sarcelles, a few kilometres from Paris proper. Sarcellitis described the prison-like feel of these *cités* that were not quite cities. Inhabited by some of the most fragile sections of the population, offered limited access to public service and situated far away from Paris proper, the *cités* did not fare well in the global economic crisis of 1973. They were stigmatised and associated with immigration; it was not long before politicians started purposefully mixing up correlation and causation, blaming social issues on the individuals who lived in the *cités* – on their ethno-racial identity, their culture, their religion. The social issues, the failing education system, the discrimination, the structural racism they encountered daily – it was all their fault.

In the 1970s and '80s, the image of the *cités* became associated with urban riot: the banlieues burned live on TV. During and after the early 1970s, a period of economic crisis with rising unemployment, skirmishes erupted in the outskirts of major French towns, and more specifically in Lyon and Paris. Local voices started to stigmatise the 'hordes' or the 'packs' of youth of Maghrebi origin.[40] The year 1981 was a turning point for the banlieue. That summer, just a few months after the election of François Mitterrand, the first left-wing president of the Fifth Republic, urban riots broke out in the Minguettes, a district on the outskirts of Lyon. At night, groups of locals, young ones mostly, fought with the police – throwing stones and mortars – and set cars ablaze. News of the riots of the Minguettes arrived in every French household, through the radio and the evening TV bulletins, and created a precedent. The banlieues were on fire, and it became a hot topic for the press. To protest police violence, neoliberalism, the unbearable racism that never went away or even, more bluntly, the absence of any hope for the future, the youth of the *banlieue-dortoir* – the negative term to describe commuters' town in French – literally set their environment alight. But their revendications went up in smoke, downplayed by the media and civil society, which focused on the graphic violence. From the 1990s onwards, riots – local or national – erupted regularly, often in reaction to police violence, and were chronicled by local, national and – at times – international press. The architecture of the *grands ensembles* played the role of an iconic background that had become clichéd. Newsclips looped on TV showing the dilapidated towers and low-rise blocks inhabited by black and brown youth, depicted as feral and violent, throwing stones at the police and threatening to burn up the capital city instead of studying at school and working hard, quietly and obediently. The myth of the banlieue was born.

The history of the banlieue is marked by violent events that triggered a spectrum of reactions, mostly repressive, from politicians and
civil society. In 1983, a series of riots in the summer, police violence
and racist killings triggered the March for Equality and Against
Racism – also known as *marche des beurs*, using the French slang term
for Arab – where seventeen individuals left Marseille in October 1983
and, thanks to coverage by the newspaper *Libération*, were welcomed
in December by a crowd of 100,000 people in Paris, at the end of their
1,500-kilometre journey. Their delegation even managed to meet
President Mitterrand. One of that year's killings had been of ten-
year-old Toufik Ouannes in the Cité des 4,000, when on the evening
of Saturday 9 July 1983 – during Ramadan – René A., galled by children lighting up bangers, took his son's air rifle and shot at them. A
few weeks after the killing, François Mitterrand undertook a 'tour' of
the banlieues, and stopped in La Courneuve. The presidential excur-
sion, which lasted for a whole three hours, and involved a mix of
sightseeing by car and helicopter – 'but [we flew] low enough to
distinguish the terrain', explained Mitterrand in the concluding press
conference – led to a new political ambition: *rehabilitation*.[41]

If the large-scale construction of *grands ensembles* had been banned
in 1973, the renovation and progressive destruction and replacement
would be the great work of the 1980s until today. The banlieue became
the towers and low-rise blocks that went down in spectacular explo-
sions, a vision of modernist architecture collapsing on itself one last
time, while in front of cameras former residents with tears in their
eyes shared their nostalgia for the years of their lives that had, literally, turned to rubble. The symbol was ambivalent: on the one hand,
it demonstrated the state's involvement in the resolution of a multi-
layered crisis that included, but was not limited to, the dereliction and
inadequacy of the architecture and urban planning of the *cités*. On the

other, it presented the destruction of the *grands ensembles* and their replacement by newer low-rise housing as the miraculous solution to the 'malady' of the banlieue. And in a more perverse way, one could also perceive the bringing down of a certain image of France's immigrant and urban identity: no more towers, no more immigrants, no more crime, no more unemployment. While these urban renewal programmes are carried out with good intentions, we see here the equivocal heritage of the social hygiene movement and its murkier aspects.

Summer of 2023, Cité des 4,000. Or what is left of it. I leave the RER station, take a wrong turn – of course – go back, climb a few steps and walk down Rue Honoré de Balzac. Almost all the former *barres* and towers had been named after renowned painters, musicians and writers: Debussy, Verlaine, Renoir, Ravel – but also the unavoidable Robespierre, of course. On this street stood two low-rise blocks, destroyed in 2010 and 2011. The buildings of the iconic *cité* have been progressively brought down starting in 1986, just three years after the new *rehabilitation* mantra of Mitterrand. On Sunday 19 June 2005, eleven-year-old Sidi Ahmed was killed by a stray bullet here – a brawl between two families of the *cité*. In a visit the following day, Nicolas Sarkozy, then minister of the interior, promised to 'wipe out the *cité* with a Kärcher' – a brand known in France for its high-pressure water guns used for the deep cleaning of buildings. Today the Rue Balzac is lined with mostly new buildings constructed in the last decade. Boring, unambitious architecture, but new and decent looking. I continue my journey, following the traces of the old Cité des 4,000.

All suburban towns are different, with their own histories, their own identities – different communities. What unites them is the miscellaneous architectures, the quirkiness and the unexpected encounters. La Courneuve does not disappoint. At the end of Rue Balzac I come across houses that seem to belong to the countryside more than a city known for its modernist architecture. They stand on their own, by a business park. Then on Rue Wangarĩ Muta Maathai – named after a Kenyan political and environmental activist – an old chalet and an apple tree mark the entrance to a timber shop. I walk towards La Tour – the Tower. That is the simple name given to the last-standing high-rise of the 4,000. It sits, grand, next to the Barre Fontenay. The latter is earmarked for destruction by the end of the 2020s while La Tour, already renovated, is meant to remain. I do not want to romanticise *grands ensembles* as an architectural form. But as I am standing by the proud tower built in 1963, with the faded low-rise block Fontenay in the distance, I have to acknowledge the grandeur, the ambition invested in these projects from an urban design point of view. They stand witness to another way to design cities, one to enjoy from a bird's-eye view perhaps, not one you'd necessarily want to call home. But I can't help thinking the same design in the heart of Paris, inhabited by a mix of social classes, would have had a very different, brighter future. Like everything, the modernist architecture of the banlieue, inhabited by working-class people and immigrants, is despised and ignored while, for instance, the buildings of architects Jean Dubuisson and Michel Holley in central Paris are saved, maintained, enhanced and lauded, despite their structural and conceptual issues and the cost of their maintenance.

I walk under the sad-looking, worn-out *barre* Fontenay, where some of the windows have already been blocked out with anti-squatting devices, and join Rue Lucienne – made of detached houses, with front yards and back gardens. Like most of what I have seen of La Courneuve, this place is not wealthy. I observe two neatly dressed individuals – crimson lipstick and Chanel-inspired jacket for her;

taupe suit, patent shoes and slicked hair for him – going up and down the street leafletting mailboxes. She carries a tote bag branded with the name of a well-known national estate agent. They reach the end of the street, the one by the *barre*, but don't go further than that, obviously – social housing is not for sale. '*Voilà, c'est finiii!*' I sense relief when they put their ad in the last mailbox and get in their car to go back to wherever their main office is. Even La Courneuve has the target of gentrification on its back.

France is a colour-blind country, in case you did not know. *Liberté, Égalité, Fraternité.* All brothers: the French Revolution did not like sororities. France has no 'race' or 'ethnic group'. You are not Black, or South Asian – you are French. And implicitly, if you are French, you are expected to be white.

In France, ethno-racial identities are not officially a thing, and it is also illegal to collect such data. You cannot design a research protocol using census records to evaluate whether French nationals with an Asian background have a higher tendency to own the home they live in – something you can do with a few clicks in the United Kingdom, for instance. The only variable that sheds some light on issues of racial discrimination is your country of birth and that of your parents. To use such figures is legal, and the datasets exist. So you can make a map that shows where people who were born in Turkey live in the Paris region. But if their children and grandchildren were born in France, and are thus French citizens, then you cannot measure whether they, in turn, live in segregated spaces or suffer from discrimination.

Spatial segregation based on country of origin and ethno-racial groups exists in the Paris region, which hosts about 40 per cent of all immigrants in France. As I have already discussed in this chapter, immigrants – may they be Bretons in the 1850s or Moroccans in the 1980s – tend to live close to a network of people that have the same language, religion, cuisine and hobbies, in order to maximise opportunities and benefit from the existing cultural infrastructure that connects to one's origin. If you do not speak Italian, are moving to Milan and have a distant cousin there, that relative will be your first point of call – especially if you need to find work urgently and know you might face a hostile environment when reaching your destination.

Yet Paris *cités* are not ghettos. They might have a higher density of immigrants or more immigrant communities than central Paris does, but the overall level of ethno-racial concentration is lower in France than in the United Kingdom, for instance, and much lower than in American cities.[42] The debate has been raging for several decades now among social scientists on the pertinence of describing *cités* as 'ghettos'. I side with those who say that describing the French banlieue with the words 'ghettos' or 'apartheid' only further stigmatises the people who live there and is useful only to certain politicians, journalists and polemists who, tapping into the profoundly rooted idea that all *français* are white, wish to send those people 'back home', purposefully forgetting that they are French citizens.

This should not be an excuse to ignore existing correlations between space and social and ethno-racial segregation in Paris, but tread carefully when you hear a politician or a journalist start talking of ghettos, apartheid or communitarianism. Never forget the real ghettos in Paris are the districts and banlieues where the super-rich live among themselves.

The Zone and the banlieue are myths. They comprise a diversity of spaces and identities, and it is nigh impossible to sketch their definitive sociological or demographical portraits, because it would imply drawing statistical boundaries – while myths have none. But if we simplify the idea of a *cité*, temporarily disconnecting it from its architectural form to define it as a neighbourhood where populations are struggling with multifaceted socioeconomic issues, we could use an urban unit known as *quartier politique de la ville* (QPV) to make a comparison between the banlieue and the rest of the Parisian metropolitan area. QPV are designed to pinpoint those communities that are struggling the most, in order to come up with policies to support them. Their statistics are, therefore, necessarily worse than for the rest of France's neighbourhoods. More than 1 million people live in QPV in the Greater Paris area, twice as many as in the rest of France. Unemployment is ten percentage points higher than in the rest of the Greater Paris area; 44 per cent of the population does not have a diploma, against 18 per cent in Paris; 6 per cent of households have six family members or more, against 2.3 per cent in the Greater Paris area; close to 85 per cent rent their homes, against 57 per cent in Paris; immigrants compose 35 per cent of the population, against 22.6 per cent in Paris; and finally, 22 per cent of those aged sixteen to twenty-five years old are not in school and are without a job, while that figure is just at 12 per cent in the Paris Metropolitan Area. It is when we connect the percentage of inhabitants living in a QPV to the general population of a given town that the geography of inequality across Paris percolates. And thus, while only 6.6 per cent of Parisians live in a *quartier politique de la ville* – and twelve arrondissements do not have any – 87 per cent of inhabitants of La Courneuve live in a QPV. The figure is 85 per cent in Grigny, 74 per cent in Sarcelles, 73 per cent in Clichy-sous-Bois, 71 per cent in Saint-Denis, and the long list continues . . .[43] All these place names are associated with the *grands ensembles*, with the *cités*, with all the clichés that make up the myth of the banlieue but which – I insist – should not be reduced to a single architectural form, prejudice of specific communities and other expressions of simplistic preconceptions.

Covid-19 once again revealed, to those who care to look, the social and ethno-racial inequalities that structure the Paris region. Seine-Saint-Denis, the country's poorest *département* and the one with the highest number of immigrants in its population, experienced the highest rate of excessive death from coronavirus in mainland France. Paris's 'essential workers', which the country cherished and applauded during the successive lockdowns before relegating them once again at the margins of society, are mainly immigrants. And while they already faced unequal access to health infrastructure because of their national origins and social status, they also suffered an excessive death rate in 2020 in comparison to Parisians born in France.[44]

Across France, the death rate increased by 22 per cent for those born in France, 54 per cent for French residents born in Maghreb and 114 for people living in France born in African countries but outside of Maghreb.[45] The structural inequalities, intimately connected to urban planning, architecture, and France's colonial past, that constitute the space of today's Paris, are permanent, discreet but extremely powerful expressions of racial violence.

I often think of Fâtiha, the teenager interviewed by Monique Hervo whose testimony I cited earlier. She was thirteen in 1961, a few years older than my own mother. Maybe she had children – they could be my age, or my older sister's. Maybe she had grandchildren – the age of my nephew, the age of my son. I do not know the way memory is transmitted in Algerian families: the war for independence, life before coming to France, the persecutions, Nanterre. I know, though, that

the scars of the past, the trauma, the spirits, are always passed on —
whether spoken out loud or kept in silence. In the bodies, in the souls
of her descendants, which might live somewhere in Paris or anywhere
in the world, live the ghosts of the *bidonville* and the sufferings of a
lifetime.

Conclusion

The gunshot of a Sig-Sauer SP 2022, the semi-automatic pistol used by the French police, makes a dry, high-pitched, short sound. In the video that shows the killing of Nahel Merzouk, a seventeen-year-old French Algerian shot dead in Nanterre by a police officer on 27 June 2023, the gunshot comes as a sonic puncture, the instant expulsion of metal, gunpowder and fire that took away the life of a teenager.

The video depicts two motorcycle policemen with their helmets on, one with his gun pointed directly at the driver. It is difficult to make out what they are saying. In the current audio analysis provided by the police, the policeman is meant to shout, 'Coupe', as in 'Turn off [the engine]', and then, 'Mains derrière la tête', 'Put your hands behind your head'. Others hear 'Shoote-le', 'Shoot him', followed by 'Je vais te mettre une balle dans la tête', 'I'm going to put a bullet in your head'. The latter version would change the nature of the crime, from manslaughter to murder.

A series of investigations, by the police and NGOs, are still under-way as we go to press.[1] In their initial version of the events, the police officer and his colleague explained that the shooter had opened fire to protect their lives, threatened by Merzouk driving his car at them. But the amateur video recorded by a bystander revealed that at no point was the shooter's life, or that of his colleague, threatened. The car was stopped, with the police officers standing to the side of it. No pedestrian seemed to be in immediate danger; Merzouk and the two passengers of the car were unarmed. The police had lied, once again. The police had killed, once again. The police had lied about killing a French Arab, once again. And if it was not for the video, we may never have heard of Nahel Merzouk's killing, and the riots that followed all across the country would not have erupted.

This is not the conclusion I had in mind for this book. But it happened in the last weeks of my writing, and I could not keep my

Flowers and messages left by the signpost where the car drove by Nahel Merzouk crashed after he was shot by a policeman on 27 June 2023. In the background on the left, the buildings built in the 1970s to host the prefecture and the court of Justice.

A few hundred metres from the site of Merzouk's killing, in a
bland piazza by the windows of an office canteen, a memorial
dedicated to those who died on 17 October 1961.

mind off it: another killing of another French young man of Maghrebi
origin that lived in the suburbs of Paris, another lie from the police,
another cycle of riots. When Franco-Algerian Merzouk was killed in
Nanterre – a few streets away from the old *bidonville* – as I was writing my last chapter, the words of Abbâs the Good Man, cited by
Monique Hervo, came back to me: 'It's like in Algeria, if you run
they'll shoot you down.'[2] Merzouk joined a long and sad litany of
names of African origin that met a violent death in connection to
police encounters: Mohamed Diab, killed in the Versailles police
station with a machine gun in 1972; Lahouari Ben Mohamed, shot
dead during a traffic stop by a CRS in Marseille in 1980; Malik
Oussekine, beaten to death by CRS in Paris in 1986; Youssef Khaïf,
shot dead in Mantes-la-Jolie in 1991; Zyed Benna (seventeen years

old) and Bouna Traoré (fifteen), both of whom died in a transformer while hiding from the police in Clichy-Sous-Bois in 2005; Adama Traoré, died in custody in a police station of the Paris region in 2016. These deaths are but a few on a long list that directly led to protests and riots in France over the past fifty years.

French policing is built on violence. Police officers are traditionally armed with lethal weapons and in charge of the state's repression of its citizens. This is different from, for instance, the British model of 'policing by consent' in which officers are traditionally not armed and are part of the community they police, which they patrol on foot. The former model of repression and violence, at the heart of French policing traditions, has been mixed with a racism that is profoundly rooted in French culture – in our spoken and visual languages, in the space and architecture of our cities, in the education system, in our administration and in our health system.

French policing, and more broadly the systemic racism at the heart of French society, has been the subject of repetitive, high-profile, direct criticism – including by France's ombudsman and the United Nations' Committee on the Elimination of Racial Discrimination. But nothing changes, because France is 'colour-blind'. This position, though laudable in principle, forbids any sound research on discrimination and prevents the design of solid policy to tackle it.

In reaction to the riots that followed Nahel Merzouk's death – or, to be more precise, the riots that followed the video showing the policemen had lied about the teenager's death – the two most powerful police unions published a press release on 30 June 2023 that called 'to force' these 'hordes of savages' to 'calm down'. The 'police family' should get into the fight against this 'vermin' (*nuisibles*), they wrote, before warning the government – approaching the threat of sedition

– that they would not back down. They concluded, in bold characters: 'Today, police officers are fighting because we are at war. Tomorrow we will start the resistance and the government will have to take notice.' Far-right ideas and culture have become dominant in French politics, and this press release is just one recent expression of this profound evolution.

In 1991, there was Jacques Chirac (then mayor of Paris), who denounced 'the noise and the smell' of 'Muslim and Black' polygamous families living in social housing.

There was the right-wing presidential candidate Nicolas Sarkozy announcing in 2005 he would clean the *cités* with a Kärcher.

There was the socialist president François Hollande, who presented to parliament an amendment to the constitution that would have made possible the loss of citizenship for French-born citizens holding two passports. In the context of the Paris terrorist attacks of November 2015, this was clearly aimed at French citizens also holding passports from Northern African countries, implicitly doubting their loyalty to France and French values. This constitutional change would have de facto created two categories of citizens, a breach of the constitution's most fundamental principles. It was the only time I cried in politics, out of disappointment and rage seeing a left-leaning government trying to turn into law one of the far right's wildest dreams.

Recently it was Emmanuel Macron's minister of the interior, Gérald Darmanin, using the word *ensauvagement* in a series of interviews: a concept widely used in right-wing and far-right circles arguing that society is going backwards to a state of 'savagery' and losing the principles of 'civilisation'. These interventions – among many others – imply that immigrants, but also the children and grandchildren of immigrants, are of lesser moral and human qualities. Implicitly, it presents immigrants and their descendants as 'bad' people, as dishonest, duplicitous, savages, barbarians, wild beasts, vermin, pests.

This focus on immigration is not on *all* immigrants, it is not on those who have names from Italy, Spain or Hungary. It is on those immigrants and descendants of immigrants with darker skin colours and names from Tunisia, Morocco, Senegal, Ivory Coast, Mali, Sudan and so on. Such discourse ensures the continuation of racist constructions connected to colonialism, which the majority of French politicians and top civil servants refuse to tackle, or even to acknowledge. Instead, these actions, these words, actively or passively become the fuel for the perpetuation and accentuation of racism and hatred, in a country where far-right parties, at each election, come closer to taking hold of the supreme power.

What I aimed to touch upon in this book is the role urbanism and architecture played in the construction of the Other in the context of Paris, and how the opposition of 'Paris versus banlieue' crystallised this Otherness in space. The Other might be an administrative status (immigrant), an ethno-racial identity (Jew, Roma, Maghrebi, African), an origin, a class, a political affiliation (Communist), a trade (ragpicker) or the conditions determined by one's neighbourhood or the state of one's home: a Parisian slum or a *bidonville*.

Even though I have left these categories out of this book because I think their geographies and architectures are connected to different social-spatial dynamics, one might also be Other because of gender or sexuality. Often, these identities and categories intersect, or they have been deliberately mixed together to imply correlation: Jews in the dilapidated buildings of the Marais, ragpickers in the Zone, Northern Africans in the *bidonvilles* – these groups lived as they lived, it was argued, because it was their social and ethno-racial natures. They were born as such; their genes, their race predestined them to this fate – it was not French society's responsibility, but theirs and theirs alone.

In creating this Otherness, one establishes a dichotomy between the 'us' and the 'them'. It is then up to individuals to self-identify as belonging to the 'us' or the 'them', even though their perception might end up proven wrong by history – for instance, when secular Jews with French roots going back several generations were deported by French police. They realised too late they had remained the 'them'. The 'them' is foreign; the 'us' is *proper*: well-bred, well-dressed, white, probably Christian, male and straight, with savings accounts.

The myth of the banlieue, the idea of the *cités* is the latest form of the archetypal and spatialised construction of the Other – an association between an architecture and its landscape (high-rise modernism), a set of ethno-racial identities (African and Maghrebi), a religion (Islam), in a difficult socio-economic context with high rates of unemployment and poverty. The ensemble of these characteristics constitutes a socio-spatial caricature that has just enough truth in it to be perpetually rebooted by the media and political leaders.

The banlieues and the immigrants have become, at least since the global economic crisis of 1970s, the scarecrows of France's public spheres. The Other has its own neighbourhoods – as seen on TV. But there is one major difference in the *cités*, which is once again connected to urban policy and land use: unlike the Zone that remains so present in Paris's imaginary, unlike the Marais when it was considered a slum, you rarely go to these remote banlieue that have nothing to offer – except homes, of course, for those that inhabit them.

They are residential districts with nothing to visit, except a friend or a relative. One does not go to the *cités* for cheap wine and entertainment, as one did in the Zone. One never walks through it by chance or visits it to see some crumbling but distinctive architectural features, or shop in a specific grocery store as one might have done in the Marais when it was a poor, dilapidated – but very central – neighbourhood. The spatial typology of the *grands ensembles*, built outside cities' historic footprints, reinforce their exclusionary dimensions – not only because they impose long commuting times on their residents, but also because their remoteness removes them permanently from being actors in the public life of the city.

It is highly likely that an average French person – I am not even mentioning foreigners and tourists – only ever had access to a mediated experience of the *cités*, even if one lives a few RER stops from them. They would have acquired an experience of these spaces through the media, the politicians and other cultural artefacts: from feature movies to literature, photography to music. This distance reinforces the Otherness and, even more, the *exoticism* associated with the *cités*, while a juxtaposition with perceived violence achieves their marginalisation as no-go zones. Their differences, their characters and those of their inhabitants are erased to create stereotypical spaces inhabited by clichéd communities that are implicitly or explicitly depicted as barbarians living in uncivilised conditions.

The stories I recounted in this book have focused on the intermixing of social programmes, architecture and policing. Because spatial design is always political. None of the philosophies of urban planning that have guided urbanists, prefects and mayors in the organisation of Paris's space were neutral – though some of them could be equivocal, such as social hygiene. It is important to bear in mind the necessary political nature of architecture and urban planning when apprehending any urban project – then and now.

If temporal distance and the works of historians help us critique the ideals of yesterday's planners, we should not fool ourselves into

believing that today's urbanism is more neutral, objective or scientific
than in the past – even when sugar-coated with the veneer of 'sustain-
ability' or 'green urbanism'. Urban policy remains a form of control,
law enforcement and 'peacekeeping'. In the July 2023 cabinet reshuf-
fle, which was not a direct consequence of the Merzouk's riots but
followed them, the portfolio of urban affairs – which has been a
minor, if not neglected topic during Macron's and Hollande's successive terms – has been given to a junior minister with no prior experience of urban policy. Most importantly, for the first time since the
appointment of a minister for urban affairs in 1990 during François
Mitterrand's second presidential term, the Junior Ministry for Urban

The Porte de Montreuil in 2013, displaying the horizontal layers of
Paris urbanism. From top to bottom, the fabric of Paris; the Pink
Belt; the remnants of the Green Belt (stadia, playgrounds, etc.), the
Boulevard Périphérique, the suburban towns of Montreuil and Bagnolet
with the flea market, followed by urban planning intervention of the
1980s and the loose, low-density, historic fabric of suburban towns.

Affairs was placed under the supervision of the minister of the interior, Gérald Darmanin. In Macron's vision, urban policy has become an issue directly and openly pertaining to police and security, instead of economic development or spatial justice.

From a specific place in the history of Paris, the Zone is today evolving slowly into an abstract space. The 'dirt belt' of the ring road will eventually fade away, soothed by processes of gentrification that will see the frontiers of 'properness' extend beyond the municipal borders of the City of Paris. The price of a home still drops by 30 per cent as soon as you cross the Boulevard Périphérique, but not for long.

Plans to turn the former Zone into a new 'green belt', in connection with the Summer Olympics of 2024 and the cortege of money poured into new accommodations, roads and other infrastructure, together with the vast construction programmes of new *métro* lines across the Paris region, will further densify the urban fabric of Paris. It will reduce commuting times, provide new homes and increase the accessibility of some districts and suburban towns that took longer to reach from central Paris than many provincial towns with high-speed train connections. It will also increase tremendously the price of real estate, pricing out other sections of French society.

The Olympics, the new *métro*, will change the geography of Paris – it will contribute to expanding the urban area, finally pushing further away the boundaries of a city whose symbolic space has not changed since the nineteenth century. But the Zone will not disappear. The belts of Paris will not disappear. Because the social and political matrix of the city, its deep infrastructure, will not change. The Zone will move, it will morph, and the strategies of exclusion that have made Paris the city it is today will repeat, fuelled by a renewed logic of neoliberalism that has become the prevalent mode of city planning. The spatial design of Paris will remain connected to the making of the Other, articulated to fabricate an opposition between an idealised 'us' and an imagined 'them'. The journey of the Zone continues.

Acknowledgements

This book is the result of a long journey of many years. Not its writing per se, but the journey that made the writing possible. The learning of a language, English, that I love. The distant relationship I have built with my beloved hometown of Paris. A PhD on its ring road provided me with plenty of excuses to go back and forth between London and France. It has been a long route, where I met plenty of friends – some foes too – who would deserve to be listed here, if it was not for the ink and paper my affection for them would consume. For sharing their love of Paris, for being at my side always, thank you to my parents and sister. My love goes to my partner Cécile for her support all these years, and for setting me up to live in London for a decade. Many kisses on our son's plump cheeks. Odilon, you make our lives always more joyful and eventful. And to my partner's family for their kindness.

I would like to thank Leo Hollis of Verso for his impeccable editorial direction, precise edits and almost painless cuts. It has been a great pleasure to work with him on my first book. Thanks to the team at Verso for all their work: Conor O'Brien for the precise copy-editing and production editor Nick Walther. Thank you to the friends who have agreed to read my first draft – even if their crazy busy lives have not always allowed them to send me feedback in time! – Jordan Rowe, Lucie Trémolières, George Kafka, Meriem Chabani, Enora Robin and Cécile Trémolières. Thank you to the whole team at *Flaneur* – I was delighted to join them for their ninth issue dedicated to the Boulevard Périphérique, and their energy and creativity accompanied me in the crafting of this book. And finally, thank you to those who have shared, in their personal or professional capacity, their knowledge and memories: Annick Prime, Vincent Tuchais, David Madden, Lucie Lapuszanska, among others.

Notes

Introduction

1   The neighbourhoods in Pantin and Aubervilliers that are right next to the park are among the poorest 5 per cent of Région Île-de-France, and France's poorest 10 per cent.

1 Black Belt

1   Jean-Louis Cohen and André Lortie, *Des fortifs au périf: Paris, les seuils de la ville* (Paris: Éditions du Pavillon de l'Arsenal, 2020), 22.

2   Patricia O'Brien, 'L'Embastillement de Paris: The Fortification of Paris during the July Monarchy', *French Historical Studies* 9 (1975): 63–82.

3   Nathalie Montel, *Faire le Grand Paris: Avis des habitants consultés en 1859*, Mémoire commune (Rennes; Paris: Presses universitaires de Rennes; Comité d'histoire de la ville de Paris, 2012).

4   David Harvey, *Paris: Capital of Modernity* (New York; London: Routledge, 2003), 2.

5   Kristin Ross, *The Emergence of Social Space: Rimbaud and the Paris Commune* (London, New York: Verso, 2008), 41.

6   Cited in Pierre Pinon, *Atlas du Paris Haussmannien* (Paris: Parigramme, 2016), 92.

7   Ibid., 92.

8   Ibid., 93.

9   Sandra Brée, 'La population de la région parisienne au xixe siècle', in *Paris, l'inféconde: La limitation des naissances en région parisienne au xixe siècle*, Études et Enquêtes Historiques (Paris: Ined Éditions, 2020), 59–93.

10   Chagot, *La Rue de Rivoli Prolongée*, 4 March 1854.

11   Christiane Demeulenaere-Douyère, 'L'annexion vue de l'Est parisien: Inquiétudes, espérances et insatisfactions . . .', in *Agrandir Paris (1860–1970)*, ed. Annie Fourcaut and Florence Bourillon (Paris: Éditions de la Sorbonne, 2012), 138.

12   Montel, *Faire le Grand Paris*, 101.

13   Madeleine Leveau-Fernandez, 'La dernière enceinte de Paris, 1840–1970' (Université de Paris-VII, 1983).

14   Cited in Cohen and Lortie, *Des fortifs au périf*, 63–4.

15   Stéphanie Tonnerre-Seychelles, 'Grandeur et misère des chiffonniers de Paris (1/2)', *Le Blog Gallica* (blog), 25 May 2020.

16   Léon Colin, *Paris, sa topographie, son hygiène, ses maladies* (Paris: G. Masson, 1885), 259.

17   Alexandre Privat d'Anglemont, *Paris anecdote* (Paris: P. Jannet, 1854), 217.

18   1895 article by Émile Chizat, cited in Jérôme Beauchez, *Les sauvages de la civilisation* (Paris: Éditions Amsterdam, 2022), 46.

19   Georges-Eugène Haussmann, *Mémoires* (Paris: Seuil, 2000), 556.

20   Walter Benjamin, *Illuminations*, ed. Hannah Arendt, trans. Harry Zohn (New York: Schocken Books, 1968), 226.

21   Eugène Atget, *Poterne des peupliers*, 1913.

22   Eugène Atget, *Porte de Montreuil*, 1912.

23   Eugène Atget, *Porte de Montreuil*, 1913.

2 Green Belt

1   Hillary Angelo, *How Green Became Good: Urbanized Nature and the Making of Cities and Citizens* (Chicago: University of Chicago Press, 2021).

2   Martin Nadaud cited in Cohen and Lortie, *Des fortifs au périf*, 66.

3   Justinien Tribillon, 'London Is the Place for Me', in *A City of Comings and Goings*, ed. Crimson (Rotterdam: nai010, 2019), 72.

4   Élisée Reclus, 'The Evolution of Cities', *The Contemporary Review* (February 1895).

5   Eugène Hénard, 'Une Ceinture de parcs pour Paris à l'emplacement des fortifications', *L'Architecture*, April 1909.

6   Eugène Hénard, 'Les espaces libres et les fortifications. Le projet Dausset et le projet du Musée Social', *L'Architecture*, 11 December 1909.

7   Marie Charvet, *Les fortifications de Paris. De l'hygiénisme à l'urbanisme, 1880–1919* (Rennes: Presses Universitaires de Rennes, 2005).

8   Hénard, 'Les espaces libres', 422.

9   Hénard, 'Une ceinture', 135.

10   Hénard, 'Les espaces libres', 420.

11   Agence Nationale pour la Rénovation Urbaine, 'Présentation de l'ANRU'.

12   Marlène Ghorayeb, 'La loi Cornudet, un urbanisme hygiéniste et social', *Droit et Ville* 88, no. 2 (2019): 43–58.

13   Frédérique Audoin-Rouzeau, *Chapitre VIII. L'argument épidémiologique des foyers familiaux* (Presses universitaires de Rennes, 2003).

14   All citations are taken from the minutes of the debate, translated by the author, 'Compte Rendu in Extenso de La 7e Séance, Séance Du Jeudi 2 Décembre 1920', *Journal Officiel*, 3 December 1920, 1837–49.

15   Éric Alonzo, *L'architecture de la voie* (Marseille & Champs-sur-Marne: Parenthèses Éditions & École de la ville et des territoires, 2018).

16   François Chaslin, *Le Corbusier* (Paris: Seuil, 2015).

17   Dorothée Imbert, 'Vichy vert: Les paysagistes entre technique et terroir', in *Architecture et urbanisme dans la France de Vichy*, ed. Jean-Louis Cohen, Conférences (Paris: Collège de France, 2020), 107–24.

18   'L'armistice du 25 Juin 1940', *Revue des deux mondes (1829–1971)* 58, no. 1 (1940): 5–11.

19   Maurice Baudot and Ch.-J. Reverdy, 'Le programme d'équipement sportif dans le département de la Seine', *Technique et architecture*, October 1941, 32.

20   André Vera cited in Imbert, 'Vichy vert'.

21   André Véra, 'Pour le renouveau de l'art français: Le jardin', *Urbanisme*, 1943, 1.

22   André Véra cited in Imbert, 'Vichy vert'.

23   Gert Groening and Joachim Wolschke-Bulmahn, 'Some Notes on the Mania for Native Plants in Germany', *Landscape Journal* 11, no. 2 (1992): 116–26.

24   Inspecteur général chef des services techniques de topographie et d'urbanisme, 'La voirie parisienne projet d'aménagement de la Ville de Paris' (Paris: Ville de Paris, 1943).

3 Pink Belt, Red Belt

1   Romain Gustiaux, 'L'empreinte de la Grande Guerre sur le logement social en France (1912–1928)', *Revue d'histoire de la protection sociale* 9, no. 1 (2016): 88–109.

2   Le Corbusier cited in Cohen and Lortie, *Des fortifs au périf*, 155.

3   Cendrars, 1949, in ibid., 179.

4   Emmanuel Bellanger, *Ivry, banlieue rouge. Capitale du communisme français, XXème siècle* (Grâne: Créaphis, 2017).

5   Bellanger, *Ivry, banlieue rouge*, 87.

6   Robert Chenevoix, 'Les communistes à Ivry – Manifestation manquée', *Le Figaro*, 6 August 1928, gallica.bnf.fr.

7   'Au Cirque de Paris, 10 000 travailleurs crient "À Ivry!"', *L'Humanité*, 5 August 1928.

8   Jean-Louis Cohen, 'L'école Karl Marx à Villejuif (1930–1933)', in *Banlieue rouge 1920–1960*, ed. Annie Fourcaut (Paris: Autrement, 1982), 197–206.

9   Annie Fourcaut, *Bobigny, banlieue rouge* (Paris: Éditions de l'Atelier, 1989).

10   Emmanuel Bellanger, 'De de Gaulle à Pompidou, lorsque l'État s'opposait aux élus locaux: l'exemplarité du Grand Paris', in *Le grand dessein parisien de Georges Pompidou. L'aménagement de Paris et de la région capitale*, ed. Philippe Nivet et al. (Paris: Somogy, 2010), 43–53.

11   Michel Brisacier, 'Paris dans la pensée et l'action de Charles de Gaulle' (Thèse de doctorat, Paris 1, 1986), 662.

4 Dirt Belt

1   Antoine Picon, 'French Engineers and Social Thought, 18–20th Centuries: An Archeology of Technocratic Ideals', *History and Technology* 23, no. 3 (September 2007): 197–208.

2   Philippe Nivet, *Le Conseil municipal de Paris de 1944 à 1977*, Histoire de la France aux XIXe et XXe siècles (Paris: Éditions de la Sorbonne, 1994).

3   Barry Allen, *Artifice and Design: Art and Technology in Human Experience* (Ithaca: Cornell University Press, 2008), 19.

5 Rust Belt, White City

1   Julia Pascual, 'Au centre de rétention administrative de Vincennes, des tensions croissantes', *Le Monde*, 14 July 2023; 'Mort d'un migrant au centre de rétention de Vincennes', *Le Monde*, 26 May 2023.

2   Emmanuel Blanchard, 'L'internement avant l'internement Commissariats, centres de triage et autres lieux d'assignation à résidence (il)-légale', *Matériaux pour l'histoire de notre temps* 92, no. 4 (2008): 8–14.

3   Louisa Yousfi, *Rester barbare* (Paris: La Fabrique, 2022).

4   Jean Royer, ed., *L'urbanisme aux colonies et dans les pays tropicaux* (La Charité-sur-Loire: Delayance, 1932), 7.

5   Lyautey cited in Jean-François Guillot, 'La Société française des urbanistes et l'Institut d'urbanisme : deux usages du réseau pour une même cause ?', in *La France savante*, ed. Arnaud Hurel, Actes des congrès nationaux des sociétés historiques et scientifiques (Paris: Éditions du Comité des travaux historiques et scientifiques, 2018), 225–33.

6   Charlotte Jelidi, 'II. Principe fondateur de l'urbanisme sous le Protectorat : séparation, ségrégation ou apartheid urbain ?', in *Fès, la fabrication d'une ville nouvelle (1912–1956)*, Sociétés, Espaces, Temps (Lyon: ENS Éditions, 2014), 57–88.

7   Henri Prost quoted in Jelidi's chapter, cited above.

8   Royer, *L'urbanisme aux colonies*, 11.

9   Ibid., 22.

10 Évelyne Cohen, 'Chapitre I. Tableaux de paris entre-deux-guerres', in *Paris dans l'imaginaire national de l'entre-deux-guerres*, Histoire de la France aux XIXe et XXe siècles (Paris: Éditions de la Sorbonne, 2016), 21–60.

11 Françoise Vergès, *De la violence coloniale dans l'espace public* (Marseille: Shed, 2021), 28.

12 Palais de la porte dorée, 'La commande architecturale du Palais de la Porte Dorée | Monument du Palais de la Porte dorée', monument.palais-portedoree.fr.

13 Frantz Fanon, *Pour la révolution africaine: écrits politiques* (Chicoutimi: J.-M. Tremblay, 2011), 168.

14 Yves Lequin, *Histoire des étrangers et de l'immigration en France*, Éd. refondue et mise à jour édition (Paris: Larousse, 2006), 396–97.

15 Samia Henni, *Architecture of Counterrevolution: The French Army in Northern Algeria* (Zurich: gta Verlag, 2017), 149–78.

16 'Après la mort de cinq Africains à Aubervilliers', *Le Monde*, 7 January 1970.

17 Abdelmalek Sayad, *Un Nanterre algérien, terre de bidonvilles*, Autrement. Série Monde (1989) (Paris: Autrement, 1995), 24.

18 Ibid., 28–9.

19 Raffaele Cattedra, 'Bidonville : paradigme et réalité refoulée de la ville du XXe siècle', in *Les mots de la stigmatisation urbaine*, ed. Jean-Charles Depaule, Les mots de la ville (Paris: Éditions de la Maison des sciences de l'homme, 2017), 123–63.

20 Monique Hervo, *Nanterre en guerre d'Algérie: chroniques du bidonville: 1959–1962* (Paris: Actes Sud, 2012).

21 Ibid., 105.

22 Sayad, *Un Nanterre algérien*, 45.

23 Ibid., 99.

24 Ibid., 83.

25 Ibid., 102.

26 Hervo, *Nanterre en guerre d'Algérie*, 67.

27 Ibid., 87.

28 Ibid., 93.

29 Ibid., 113.

30 Ibid., 117.

31 Ibid., 114.

32 Ibid., 179–80.

33 Sabine Effosse, 'Chapitre II. Le logement dans l'immédiat après-guerre : une priorité secondaire, 1945–1949', in *L'invention du logement aidé en France : L'immobilier au temps des Trente Glorieuses*, Histoire économique et financière – XIXe–XXe (Vincennes: Institut de la gestion publique et du développement économique, 2013), 119–200.

34 Ibid.

35 Jean-Marc Stébé, *Le logement social en France (1789 à nos jours)* (France: PUF, coll. Que sais-je?, 7e éd., 2016), 83.

36 Annie Fourcaut, 'La construction des grands ensembles: Reconquérir Paris et régé-
    nérer la banlieue', in *Agrandir Paris (1860–1970)*, ed. Annie Fourcaut and Florence
    Bourillon (Paris: Éditions de la Sorbonne, 2012).

37 Jean-Philippe Dedieu, 'Sebastião Salgado: Migrant in a World of Migrants', Lens
    Blog, 1393495221.

38 France, 'Arrêté du 27 mars 1954 attribution des logements d'HLM: Situation des
    demandeurs' (1954).

39 Marie-Claude Blanc-Chaléard, 'Les quotas d'étrangers en HLM: Un héritage de la
    guerre d'Algérie? Les Canibouts à Nanterre (1959–1968)', *Métropolitiques*, 2012.

40 Michelle Zancarini-Fournel, 'Généalogie des rébellions urbaines en temps de crise
    (1971–1981)', *Vingtième Siècle. Revue d'histoire* 84, no. 4 (2004): 119–27.

41 'Rencontre informelle de M. François Mitterrand, Président de la République, avec la
    presse, à la Bourse du Travail de Saint-Denis, mardi 26 juillet 1983', Vie Publique, 26
    July 1983.

42 Edmond Préteceille, 'La ségrégation ethno-raciale a-t-elle augmenté dans la métro-
    pole parisienne ?', *Revue française de sociologie* 50, no. 3 (2009): 489–519; Sonia
    Arbaci, *Paradoxes of Segregation: Housing Systems, Welfare Regimes and Ethnic
    Residential Change in Southern European Cities* (Hoboken, New Jersey: Wiley, 2019).

43 Pierre-Émile Bidoux and Nathalie Couleaud, 'Les quartiers de la politique de la ville
    en Île-de-France' (Paris: Insee Île-de-France, March 2017).

44 Solène Brun and Patrick Simon, 'L'invisibilité des minorités dans les chiffres du coro-
    navirus: le détour par la Seine-Saint-Denis', in *Inégalités ethno-raciales et pandémie de
    coronavirus*, ed. Solène Brun and Patrick Simon, De Facto (Aubervilliers: Institut des
    migrations, 2020), 68–78.

45 'Une hausse des décès deux fois plus forte pour les personnes nées à l'étranger que
    pour celles nées en France en mars-avril 2020', Insee Focus, 198.

Conclusion

1 Index and Earshot – two NGOs created by former members of Forensic Architecture,
   and using similar investigative techniques – have an ongoing inquiry into Merzouk's
   death. They have not shared their conclusions yet (August 2023), but argue that it is
   unlikely the policeman said 'derrière la tête', as in *'behind* your head', but instead
   'dans la tête', *'in* your head'.

2 In a Facebook post the day after the killing, the architect and editor of *The Funambulist*
   Léopold Lambert proposed a historic and spatial context for Merzouk's death, with
   maps comparing the location of the killing and the former bidonville. Léopold
   Lambert, 'La rage après le meurtre policier de . . .', *Facebook* (blog), 28 June 2023.

Image Credits

Page 3: Justinien Tribillon, 2021.

Page 17: Justinien Tribillon and Verso, 2024.

Page 24: Bibliothèque Nationale de France, 1843.

Page 29: Agence Rol / Bibliothèque Nationale de France, 1913.

Page 37: Eugène Atget / Bibliothèque Nationale de France, 1913.

Page 38: Eugène Atget / Bibliothèque Nationale de France, 1912.

Page 50: Eugène Hénard / *L'Architecture* / Bibliothèque de la Cité de l'Architecture et du Patrimoine, 1909.

Page 54: Frédéric Gadmer / Musée départemental Albert-Kahn, Inventory record A24494, 1920.

Page 71: Justinien Tribillon, 2021.

Page 75: Maurice-Louis Branger, 1913.

Page 81: IGN, Photothèque nationale, 1931.

Page 82: Auguste Léon / Musée départemental Albert-Kahn, Inventory record A62524S, 1929.

Page 83: Stéphane Passet / Musée départemental Albert-Kahn, Inventory record A69628XS, 1929.

Page 93: *L'Humanité* / Bibliothèque Nationale de France, 1928.

Page 107: IGN, Photothèque nationale, 1962.

Page 136: Justinien Tribillon, 2023.

Page 137: Justinien Tribillon, 2023.

Page 141: Frédéric Gadmer / Musée départemental Albert-Khan, Inventory record A65919S, 1931.

Page 142: IGN, Photothèque nationale, 1931.

Page 151: Justinien Tribillon, 2023.

Page 185: Justinien Tribillon, 2023.
Page 186: Justinien Tribillon, 2023.
Page 192: IGN, Photothèque nationale, 2013.